"Only rarely does an introductory volume on Christian liturgy manage to cover its assigned subject with both detail and grace, but this one most assuredly does just that. In her deftly written book, Conway Ireton provides all of us a very accessible and enormously appealing overview of the church's liturgical year."

Phyllis Tickle, compiler of *The Divine Hours*

"In a nanosecond world we need sane rhythms that slow us down enough to notice God in our lives. Kimberlee Conway Ireton guides the reader to a simple annual pathway—the church year. *The Circle of Seasons* takes a practical look at how the church journeys with Jesus through Advent, Christmas, Epiphany, Ordinary Time, Lent, Easter and Pentecost. Each season opens a door to deeper understanding and formation in faith. Accessible, readable and personable, *The Circle of Seasons* is a way forward for our time."

Adele Calhoun, copastor, Redeemer Community Church, Wellesley, Massachusetts, and author of *Spiritual Disciplines Handbook*

"There is so much more to the church year than Lent and Advent! Kimberlee Conway Ireton guides us on a lovely and inviting tour through the liturgical year, reminding us of the 'transformative potential' and sacredness of every season, even Ordinary Time. She artfully blends honest personal stories with practical tips on spiritual practices into an inspiring, well-written book. Her clear, simple, yet thought-provoking chapters on each season will help readers to find common ground with the church around the world, and to gain a deeper understanding of the Scripture and traditions that have shaped each season's celebrations."

Keri Wyatt Kent, author of *Breathe: Creating Space for God in a Hectic Life* and *Rest: Living in Sabbath Simplicity*

"This isn't just another book on the liturgical year. It penetrates more deeply. The author welcomes us into a different rhythm for measuring time. Rather than the cadence of our days being driven by the demands of our consumer culture, we are invited into a more human and more divinely ordinary way of life. Drawing together everyday experiences from her own life with ancient practices of the church, she charts a route to liberation from our society's frenzied busyness and crippling self-indulgence. Reader beware. This book can draw us into a life-re-creating journey."

Tim Dearborn, director, Christian Commitments Programs, World Vision International

"A useful and inspiring reexamination of how the church has always marked time and the seasons of the year from its Christian worldview. Reading Kimberlee Conway Ireton it is clear: living in the culture of Christianity is now—once again—countercultural."

Noel Anderson, executive pastor, First Presbyterian Church, Bakersfield, California

"Kimberlee Conway Ireton writes beautifully. Her stories from daily life are winsome, her reflections on God's grace are insightful, and her explanations of Christian history are clear and helpful. In a rich and deep way, with lovely prose, she illuminates the intersection of everyday life with the biblical themes connected to the church year."

Lynne M. Baab, author of *Sabbath Keeping* and *Fasting: Spiritual Freedom Beyond Our Appetites*

"I would recommend this book to any religious educators, and specifically to the women and men who teach children and adults at the parishes where I've worked. The hands-on projects are a godsend for anyone trying to make the Bible vivid to learners of any age."

Father James Harbaugh, S.J., author of *A 12-Step Approach to the Spiritual Exercises of St. Ignatius* and *A 12-Step Approach to the Sunday Readings*

"Offering simple practices built on Scripture, history and everyday life, Conway Ireton helps us participate in the rhythm of the Christian year. In so doing, we unite with Christians throughout the world and throughout the ages."

Jan Johnson, author of *Invitation to the Jesus Life* and *Spiritual Disciplines Companion*

Kimberlee Conway Ireton

○

THE CIRCLE
of SEASONS

Meeting God in the Church Year

○

IVP Books

An imprint of InterVarsity Press
Downers Grove, Illinois

InterVarsity Press
P.O. Box 1400, Downers Grove, IL 60515-1426
World Wide Web: www.ivpress.com
Email: email@ivpress.com

InterVarsity Press® is the book-publishing division of InterVarsity Christian Fellowship/USA®, a student movement active on campus at hundreds of universities, colleges and schools of nursing in the United States of America, and a member movement of the International Fellowship of Evangelical Students. For information about local and regional activities, write Public Relations Dept., InterVarsity Christian Fellowship/USA, 6400 Schroeder Rd., P.O. Box 7895, Madison, WI 53707-7895, or visit the IVCF website at <www.intervarsity.org>.

Scripture quotations, unless otherwise noted, are from the New Revised Standard Version of the Bible, copyright 1989 by the Division of Christian Education of the National Council of the Churches of Christ in the USA. Used by permission. All rights reserved.

Chapter 8, "Ordinary Time: Transfiguration," is adapted in part from an article originally published in Weavings: A Journal of the Christian Spiritual Life 21, no. 1 (January/February 2006). Copyright © 2006 by Upper Room Ministries.

Personal stories included in this book are shared by permission.

Design: Janelle Rebel
Images: Frederick Bass/Getty Images

ISBN 978-0-8308-3625-3

Printed in the United States of America ∞

InterVarsity Press is committed to protecting the environment and to the responsible use of natural resources. As a member of Green Press Initiative we use recycled paper whenever possible. To learn more about the Green Press Initiative, visit http://www.greenpressinitiative.org.

Library of Congress Cataloging-in-Publication Data

Conway Ireton, Kimberlee, 1975-
    The circle of seasons: meeting God in the church year / by
Kimberlee Conway Ireton.
        p. cm.
    Includes bibliographical references (p.   ).
    ISBN 978-0-8308-3625-3 (pbk.: alk. paper)
    1. Church year.   2. Fasts and feasts.   I. Title.
    BV30.I74 2008
    263'.9—dc22

                2008022655

P   27   26   25   24   23   22   21   20   19   18   17   16   15   14   13   12   11   10   9   8   7   6   5   4   3   2   1
Y   31   30   29   28   27   26   25   24   23   22   21   20   19   18   17   16   15   14   13   12   11   10   09   08

For the people of Bethany Presbyterian Church,
who have taught me most everything I know
about living the church year

Contents

Introduction

Entering the Circle:
The Church Year

In March of my junior year in high school, some Catholic girls in my history class, knowing I was a Christian, asked me what I was giving up for Lent.

"Lent?" My blank look told them I had no idea what they were talking about. Growing up in a predominantly evangelical environment, I did not know that the church has its own calendar, with more on it than just Christmas and Easter. I did know about Advent, because my sister and I had always opened Advent calendars in December, but Advent in my mind was just an adjective for "calendar" and was more about counting the days till Santa and gifts than about anything else, let alone preparing for the birth of Jesus.

My classmates explained that Lent begins on Ash Wednesday and is the season of preparation for Easter and that you usually observe Lent by fasting or giving something up. I decided to give something up—chocolate, I believe—though I had no understanding of why I was doing so. I rather doubt it occurred to me to ask. Still, this conversation cracked open my awareness of such a thing as a uniquely Christian way of marking time.

Two years later and a thousand miles away, I found myself at a small Presbyterian church on the Thursday before Easter for a Tenebrae service, in which the sanctuary was gradually shrouded in darkness until, at the end of the service, we stumbled in utter blackness out of the church. This descent into darkness powerfully evoked for me the horror and sadness of the crucifixion, something I had never experienced before. Suddenly Jesus' death became something that mattered in a real way, a way no amount of talking could explain. But meaningful as it was, this service was more or less an isolated event, not connected in my mind to the Lent of my junior year and high school years or the alleluias of the Easter that followed.

Two more years passed, and I discovered the nonfiction of Madeleine L'Engle, whose casual dropping of the names of holy days and church seasons finally made me realize that Lent and the Tenebrae service, Easter and Pentecost, Advent and Christmas were all of the same cloth, weaving in and out of one another to create a beautiful whole, a circle of seasons that told the story of Jesus and the story of the church. I began to take notice of what those seasons were saying, what part of the story they were telling, and to wonder how I might enter into that story, that season.

When I was twenty-five and newly married, my husband and I spent a year in central Minnesota so I could pursue graduate theological studies at St. John's University, a Benedictine school and monastery. In addition to joining the monks each weekday morning for prayer, Doug and I found ourselves worshiping on Sundays at Sacred Heart Chapel, a beautiful, white, light-filled church at the sister college of St. Benedict's a few miles away.

The sisters at St. Ben's knew how to do liturgy. Each week the priest's robes and the vestments and altar cloths changed, often for reasons I did not understand but which I knew had some connection to the Scripture, the liturgy and the season. During Easter (which I learned that year is a season, not just a day), we waited each Sunday in the large foyer outside the sanctuary until the organist began to play. Then we processed, singing, into the sanctuary behind a sister who carried the processional cross bedecked with yellow, green and peach ribbons tied at the bottoms with small bells. The procession evoked a sense of celebration and joy that was heightened by our singing and our alleluias and was reflected in the bright colors of the altar cloth and the priest's robes.

When Doug and I returned to Seattle the following year, the church we were members of had a new music minister who brought an increased level of attentiveness to our corporate observance of the church year. Or maybe it was I who had a heightened awareness of the change in mood, color and music that reflected the changing seasons of the year. Whichever it was, paying attention to the circling of the seasons has deepened my faith, grounding my life with Christ in time, in Scripture and in community.

THE STRUCTURE OF THE CHURCH YEAR

The church year, also called the Christian year or the liturgical year, is divided into two "halves." The first half, beginning in early December with the first Sunday of Advent and stretching till Pentecost in May or June, tells the story of the life of Christ. The second half, from Pentecost until Christ the King Sunday in late November, is the story of the church.

The first half of the year is when the church's most important holy days occur. It is divided into two tripartite cycles: Advent/ Christmas/Epiphany and Lent/Easter/Pentecost. In each of these cycles, a season of preparation precedes a season of celebration and concludes with a special day of rejoicing. At the end of each cycle comes a season called Ordinary Time.

The church year begins with Advent, the season of preparation for Christ's nativity. Advent culminates in the season of Christmas, when we celebrate the incarnation of Christ. Christmas ends in Epiphany, the remembrance of the coming of the magi, which is followed by the first cycle of Ordinary Time. As Advent is a season of preparation for Christmas, so Lent is a season of preparation for the celebration of Christ's resurrection during Easter. Pentecost, recalling the gift of the Holy Spirit to Christ's disciples, closes this cycle of the church year and inaugurates the second half of the year, another cycle of Ordinary Time.

Appropriately named, Ordinary Time is a long season (together, its two cycles comprise well over half the church year), reflecting the truth that we live most of our lives in the long, routine stretches of ordinary, daily life. Ordinary Time concludes with the holy day known as Christ the King, a celebration of our Lord's victorious coming at the end of time, after which we circle back again to Advent and wait for Christ's *first* coming in the form of a human baby.

The cyclical, circular nature of the church year provides us with repeated opportunities to live out various aspects of our faith, to see life through the lens of the Christ-story and to deepen our understanding of what it means to be a follower of Jesus. The church year has seasons of darkness, of light, of sorrow, of rejoicing, of just getting through. Our lives have such seasons too. By incorporating these experiences, the church year hallows them, reminding us that all time is sacred because God is present in it. If Easter this year is not particularly joyful or deeply meaningful in the way we had hoped, we have another Easter to look forward to, and another one after that! We can grow in, with and through the seasons of the church year. Some years those seasons will align with what is happening in our lives. Other years, they will not. But year after year, the seasons circle round. We can enter into them or not, but the invitation to wait, prepare, repent, celebrate, receive, rejoice is always extended.

Observing the seasons of the church year also helps us embrace the church's telling of time instead of our culture's. Our culture's calendar is grounded in capitalism, which requires consumption. Back-to-school sales, day-after-Thanksgiving sales, the Christmas shopping season, after-Christmas sales, Valentine's Day, Easter, Mother's Day, graduation, Father's Day, the Fourth of July—there is a sale associated with each and every cultural holiday or occasion to induce us to consume more. This way of measuring time reduces us to mere consumers, instead of inviting us to be fully human, with all the varied emotions, experiences and roles that entails.

The church year, on the other hand, is grounded in the story of Christ, which is the foundational story of our lives as Christians. It tells the story of our faith—the grand and sweeping story of the God who came to live among us as one of us; who lived a human life with all its attendant joys, sorrows and boredoms; who died a humiliating death; who rose triumphant from the grave; who sent his Spirit[1] to empower us to be his hands and feet, his face and voice, that all people might come to know his great love for them; who reigns in power and majesty; and who will return at

the end of history to establish justice and mete out mercy. Year
after year as the weeks circle by, we get to hear this story, we get
to tell this story, we get to live this story.

Further, the church year is necessarily communal. Its locus
is Sunday, in the weekly gathering of the faithful to celebrate
Christ's resurrection in Word and sacrament. In an individualistic
culture, this focus on community celebration is a witness to the
wholeness that people can have only in living life together.

The church year is another way God reaches into time to draw
us to himself. In living each year the mystery of our faith—
Christ has died, Christ is risen, Christ will come again—we open
ourselves to receive a deeper understanding of that mystery, a
deeper appreciation of the depth of God's sacrificial love for us, a
deeper gratitude for the manifold ways and places God works and
plays in our lives.

THE STRUCTURE OF THIS BOOK

The eight chapters of this book correspond with the eight parts
of the church year: Advent, Christmas, Epiphany, the first cycle
of Ordinary Time, Lent, Easter, Pentecost and the second cycle of
Ordinary Time. These parts of the church year vary in length—
from the one-day celebrations of Epiphany and Pentecost to the
thirty-plus-week season of Ordinary Time. I have tried, in each
chapter, to draw out themes from the lectionary readings for the
day or season under discussion. (The *Revised Common Lectionary* is a
three-year cycle of Scripture readings. For each Sunday there is
a psalm; an Old Testament passage, except during Easter when
we read from Acts; an epistle reading; and a Gospel passage.) I
have also linked the season thematically to a story, usually from
my life or the life of someone I know, in an attempt to show that

the seasons of the church year are relevant to our lives and, more importantly, that we can make sense of our lives in light of the church year.

While I speak of "the church year" as if there were one calendar for all Christians, that is not entirely accurate. The texture of the Christian year is similar throughout the world, with its focus on preparing for and celebrating Incarnation (Christmas) and Resurrection (Easter), but the length of the seasons and the dating of holy days, as well as the practices associated with them, differ in many Eastern churches from those in the West. What I am writing of in this book is primarily the Western church calendar, and even within that calendar, there are denominational differences. "The church year" is not monolithic but richly varied. I play here with the variations I know best and have found most personally meaningful.

At the end of each chapter is a section called "Living the Season," which provides two or three ideas of concrete things you can do to bring that season into your home and your life. (Other ideas are embedded in each chapter.) In this section you will also find discussion or reflection questions for the season. These questions are rooted in lectionary readings and encourage meditation on the themes of the chapter.

At the end of the book is a short list of books for further reading on the church year. As I have barely skimmed the surface of the richness that the church year holds, I hope readers will be inspired to dig deeper and learn more by reading and ingesting these other books.

Finally, I have included a brief appendix of ideas for church leaders, particularly those involved in planning and leading worship services at their churches. These are focused on the corporate aspect of Christian life and are arranged in two triads: Advent/Christmas/Epiphany and Lent/Easter/Pentecost.

My hope in writing this book is that it will encourage you to embrace the church year and find ways to live it. As with much of Christianity, the church year can be radically countercultural, a much-needed light showing a better way to live. In a culture that is too often hurried and distracted, the church year helps us pay attention because it draws our focus continually back to Christ. It hallows time, reminding us that time, too, belongs to our sovereign God, who is present in it, if only we will slow down long enough to notice.

In a culture where people often feel isolated, lonely and frag-mented, the church year calls us to community and wholeness. It was created by the body of Christ for the body of Christ, as a way of helping us point one another toward Christ. By telling the whole Christian story in all its richness year in and year out, the church year proclaims God's creative and redemptive purposes for us.

Rooted in time, in community and in the greatest, truest story of all, the church year focuses our attention, moment by moment, season by season, year after year, on the one thing that is needful, enabling us to enter together into the very life of God as he enters into life with us.

1 ∘ *Advent*

A Season of Waiting

Seven months into my first pregnancy, my belly was so big I couldn't lie down, not even on my side, so I propped myself up in bed with six pillows supporting me, to put myself in as upright a position as I could be. Sleep was, to say the least, elusive. By the ninth month I was so exhausted and achy from carrying around forty extra pounds that all I wanted was to sleep soundly for a month and wake up when the baby was ready to be born.

But my husband and I had moved to a new home six weeks before my due date, which meant I needed to unpack all our boxes and to prepare a space in our new house for the baby, not to mention for Doug and me. I also *had* to make multiple trips to Babies"R"Us, IKEA and numerous other stores to order and buy all manner of mostly unnecessary baby accouterments. Then, two weeks before Jack was born, I decided I hated the taupe walls in our house, and I hired someone to come in and paint four rooms and the stairwell. This meant moving most of the furniture, which involved repacking our book boxes and file boxes in order to move our bookcases and file cabinet away from the walls and then unpacking those same boxes a few days later, once the paint dried.

People laughed and told me I was nesting, trying to get our new home ready for the baby. In retrospect, though, I think my busyness was more about avoidance than preparation. I was so eager to not be pregnant anymore that I did not think about all the changes having a baby would wreak in my life. Our house was mostly ready for our son by the time he arrived, but I was not. Emotionally and psychologically, I was completely unprepared for the reality of a living, breathing, screaming baby for whom I was responsible. All my rushing around served only to distract me from the one thing I needed to think about and plan for: what life with Jack was going to require of me.

Liturgically, the season of Advent is to be a time similar to the weeks before a baby is born. It is a time of waiting and preparation.

THE ORIGINS OF ADVENT

The arrival of Advent marks the beginning of the church year. In the Western church, Advent begins on the fourth Sunday before Christmas. It begins somewhat earlier in Orthodox churches, usually in mid-November. The word itself is from the Latin *adventus*—coming.

Advent originated as a period of fasting in preparation for the Feast of the Nativity (Christmas), most likely in Gaul (modern-day France). This pre-Christmas fast was practiced in some form by the late 400s, though it wasn't until the second half of the sixth century, when prayers and scriptural texts for the Sundays preceding Christmas began to be written and selected, that Advent as we know it came into being. In addition to being a time of preparation for the celebration of Christ's nativity, Advent had an eschatological dimension and was therefore a time to ponder and prepare for Christ's second coming at the end of history.

Because Advent is a season of preparation and penitence, fasting has historically been part of Advent observance, a way to clear away the detritus of the year and create space in our lives for Christ to come. A recovery of this pre-Christmas fast, which could be as simple (and as difficult!) as avoiding sugar or meat in the weeks of Advent, would help us differentiate Advent from Christmas. In our culture, "Christmas" usually starts right after Thanksgiving and ends on December 26—and we eat cookies, candies and other rich things the whole month. By fasting in some way during Advent, we enter physically into the waiting and preparation that characterize this season, and we will more fully appreciate the feast of celebration that is Christmas—because we have waited for it with our bodies as well as our hearts and minds.

The penitential aspect of Advent is reflected in the traditional liturgical color of the season: purple, the color of repentance. In recent years, though, some churches have shifted to the use of blue, the color of hope. This choice emphasizes the promise Christ made in his first coming among us that he would come again, and it is a helpful reminder that in Advent we are not simply waiting for the coming of Christmas but that we are ultimately waiting for the second coming of Christ.

JOY TO THE WORLD?

Unfortunately Advent as a liturgical season focused on waiting and inward preparation has disappeared culturally; even in the church, we often ignore its call to reflection. Advent has become "the holiday season," and we measure it in the number of shopping days left before the twenty-fifth of December rolls around. We cram the weeks before Christmas with parties and shopping and decorating and the wrapping of gifts and the mailing of cards inscribed with words like "Peace on earth" or "Joy to the world," even though we too often feel anything but peaceful and joyful as we scurry around checking things off our endless to-do list. As with my busyness during the last weeks of my pregnancy, we may be preparing physically and materially for Christmas, but we seldom stop long enough to reflect on the coming of Christ into our world and to ponder what that coming will require of us.

When Jack was born, I no longer got to sleep as well as I did those last months of pregnancy, which suddenly seemed like heaven compared to the reality of a child who cried for hours each day, who nursed around the clock and who only slept an hour at a time. I felt lonely, anxious and guilty. I wanted life to go back to the way it was before Jack was born, before I got pregnant even. I wanted to hang out with my friends, to go see a movie, to go out to dinner, to not be so anxious, exhausted and frightened all the time. I had no idea life with a baby was going to be like this, and I was a wreck.

Over the course of many months, though, I adjusted to being a mom. My priorities—time to myself, time with my friends, a good night's sleep—gradually shifted. I slowly learned to enjoy spending time with my son—and to enjoy quiet time to myself while he napped. My friends still visited and were wonderfully gracious in the face of the many interruptions a baby brings to any activity or conversation. And I learned how to cope with being awakened several times a night.

Just as life with Jack required a radical change in the way I was used to living my life, so life with Christ—Emmanuel, God-with-us—will require radical change: the radical reshifting of our priorities and the reimagining of what is possible in the world now that the incarnation has irrevocably changed the reality in which we live. The coming of Christ into our midst requires that we rethink our desires and that we learn to hold them lightly, allowing the desire of God to supplant—or increase—our own desires.

If we were to observe Advent as the season of thoughtful reflection and repentance that it has traditionally been, we would have an opportunity to do just that: to rethink our priorities, to realign our lives with God's desires for us, to seek forgiveness and to start anew—the first Sunday of Advent, after all, marks the beginning of the church year. What better time to reflect, repent, receive forgiveness and so refresh our weary souls?

To spend the weeks before Christmas in this way would be radically countercultural, to be sure, but it would also serve to remind us that we are *waiting* for Christmas—and that the celebration of Christmas is worth waiting for.

WAIT

> I wait for the LORD, my soul waits,
>   and in his word I hope;
> my soul waits for the Lord
>   more than those who watch for the morning,
>   more than those who watch for the morning.
>   (Psalm 130:5-6)

Each of the four Sundays of Advent has a watchword for the day as well as a biblical figure with whom it is associated.[1] The word for the first Sunday is *wait,* and it is associated with the prophet Isaiah: "The Lord himself . . . / will give you a sign. / . . . the maiden is with child / and will soon give birth to a son / whom she will call Immanuel" (Isaiah 7:14 JB). It is this sign, this Son, for whom we wait in Advent.

Our Advent waiting occurs on two different levels. Certainly we wait for Christmas and the celebration of Christ's birth in history past, but we also wait for the risen Christ to come again. In fact, the Gospel passage for the first Sunday of Advent[2] is not the story of Jesus' birth or the annunciation or Mary's response to the angel's startling proclamation or Mary and Joseph's journey to Bethlehem. Rather, it is part of Jesus' speech about the signs of the end of the age, when we will see "'the Son of Man coming in a cloud' with power and great glory" (Luke 21:27). The church's choice of this passage speaks to me of the larger significance of Advent. Yes, it is a time of waiting and preparation leading up to Christmas—the celebration of Jesus' birth in history—but ultimately we are not waiting for Christmas; we are waiting for Christ's return.

In English, the word *wait* tends to imply passivity, maybe even boredom. But this is not the implication that Jesus would have had in mind when he spoke of his disciples waiting for his return. In Hebrew, the word for *wait* is also the word for *hope*. (Thus translators can render "Wait for the Lord" as "Hope in the Lord" with equal accuracy.) This linguistic equation of *wait* with *hope* means that, for Jesus, immersed as he was in the language of the Hebrew Bible, there is no conceptual differentiation between waiting and hoping. They are one and the same activity. This melding is especially apropos during Advent, when we wait in hopeful expectation for the return of Christ. Henri Nouwen calls this "active waiting."

Active waiting is not about *doing* lots of things. I, for instance, *did* lots of things before Jack was born. I had the active part nailed. But I was not waiting. I was so eager not to be pregnant anymore that I rushed around on needless errands designed to pass the time and to distract me from my need for reflection and true preparation. In contrast, Nouwen says, "Active waiting means to be present fully to the moment, in the conviction that something is happening where you are and that you want to be present to it. A waiting person is someone who is present to the moment, who believes that this moment is *the* moment."[3]

One of the traditions I find most helpful in cultivating this attitude of mindful attention during Advent is our family's nightly lighting of the Advent wreath.[4] Each week during Advent, we light an additional candle, proclaiming as we do so, "Jesus Christ is the Light of the world, the Light no darkness can overcome." This progressive lighting of the candles reminds us to wait with attentiveness through the darkness of December, because the Light who is coming into the world already shines in the darkness—if only we will watch and see.

PREPARE

> And you, child, shall be called the prophet of the Most High,
>   for you will go before the Lord to prepare the way,
> to give God's people knowledge of salvation
>   by the forgiveness of their sins.
> In the tender compassion of our God
>   the dawn from on high shall break upon us,
> to shine on those who dwell in darkness and the
>   shadow of death,
>   and to guide our feet into the way of peace. (Luke 1:76-79[5])

The second Sunday's word is *prepare,* and it is linked with John the Baptist, the voice "crying in the wilderness, Prepare ye the way

of the Lord" (Luke 3:4 KJV). During these weeks before Christmas
we are to be preparing a place for Christ to come into our midst.
Much of this preparation is watchfulness. "Be on guard," Jesus
says to his disciples—and to us (Luke 21:34). We are to be always
on the watch and to pray as we wait for Christ's return. As Paul
writes to the Thessalonians:

> The Day of the Lord is going to come like a thief in the night.
> It is when people are saying, "How quiet and peaceful it is"
> that sudden destruction falls on them, as suddenly as labor
> pains come on a pregnant woman; and there is no escape. . . .
> So we should not go on sleeping, as everyone else does, but
> stay wide awake. (1 Thessalonians 5:2-3, 6 NJB)

Preparation involves paying attention and staying awake,
so that the coming of Christ will not take us by surprise
and so that we will be ready and able to recognize that day
when it comes. Just as I learned how to recognize the signs
of impending labor and packed a bag for the hospital weeks
in advance of my due date, so too we as Christians are to be
paying attention to God's presence in the world and preparing
for Christ's return.

In the circle of the church year, Advent follows a long season
of Ordinary Time in which the busyness and dailyness of our
lives can distract us, making us forget to pay attention or to
remember that we are living in expectation of Christ's return.
That is why we need Advent—it reminds us to pay attention, to
be on guard, to keep watch that we might be ready for Christ
when he comes again.

REJOICE

> My soul proclaims the greatness of the Lord,
>   and my spirit rejoices in God my Savior . . .
> for the Mighty One has done great things for me,
> and holy is his name. (Luke 1:46-49[6])

The watchword for the third Sunday of Advent is *rejoice*, and it is connected with Mary whose "soul doth magnify the Lord" (Luke 1:46 KJV). This Sunday also has a different color than the other Sundays: pink, for joy. Mary's words and the change in liturgical colors remind us that this time of waiting and preparation is a joyful time, that even in the midst of fasting and penitence we can know joy because, as Mary sang in the Magnificat, "God has done great things for [us]."

In my Protestant upbringing, Mary was simply a Jewish peasant girl who was the mother of Jesus. I've since learned that Catholic and Orthodox Christians have a much richer and more symbolic understanding of Mary. They call her Theotokos, Mother of God, God-bearer. She is the symbol of humanity itself, fallen but willingly entering into a restored relationship with God through her "yes" to the angel's proclamation that she would be the mother of the Messiah. Evangelical Christians talk a lot about inviting Jesus into our hearts. Mary was the first to do this—and she invited Jesus not just into her heart, but also into her physical body. By bearing in her womb the Son of God, she made possible the incarnation and thus, later, the crucifixion and resurrection. In so doing, she turns the mourning of our fallenness into the rejoicing of our redemption. It is God who does these great things, to be sure, as Mary herself proclaims, but how great a God we serve, that he would allow us, invite us, long for us to participate in his redeeming work in the world.

For one friend of mine, the annual sending of a Christmas letter is a way she reflects on the past year, noticing with joy (and sometimes surprise) the ways God has been present and faithful in her life and also the ways she has been able to be part of God's work in her corner of the world. Receiving this annual missive, I rejoice with my friend in the great things God is doing in her and through her.

During Advent, we are to be like my friend, joyfully aware of the presence of God in our lives. Like Mary, we are to wait actively, joyfully and expectantly for the new life that has been and will be born into the world. And also like Mary, we are to be agents of this birthing. We are to bring the Light of the world into the world.

LOVE

> For God so loved the world, that he gave his only begotten
> Son. (John 3:16 KJV)

The word for the fourth and final Sunday of Advent is *love,* and it is associated with Joseph. When God's angel told him in a dream not to be afraid to marry Mary, Joseph loved his fiancée enough to make her his wife, in spite of the raised eyebrows and innuendo that would be directed his way because of her illegitimate pregnancy. He then loved as his own the son Mary bore, though the boy was neither flesh of his flesh nor bone of his bone.

As we wait, not passively but actively, for Christmas and Christ's coming, we have the opportunity, like Joseph, to see one another as the God-bearers we are and to support and love one another as we attempt to bring to birth the new life that God has planted within us. Nouwen sees this loving support not just in Joseph and Mary's relationship but also in the meeting of Elizabeth and Mary (Luke 1:39-45):

These two women created space for each other to wait. They affirmed for each other that something was happening that was worth waiting for. I think that is the model of the Christian community. It is a community of support, celebration, and affirmation in which we can lift up what has already begun in us. The visit of Elizabeth and Mary is one of the Bible's most beautiful expressions of what it means to form community, to be together, gathered around a promise, affirming that something is really happening.[7]

Mary and Elizabeth's mutual love and support points beyond itself, giving us a picture of what Christian community looks like.

In a similar way, Joseph's love for Mary and for Jesus, with its attendant self-sacrifice, points beyond itself, giving us a glimpse of God's great outpouring of himself in love for all of us, love that is seen so clearly in the incarnation, the coming of the God who created the cosmos to live among us as one of us.

As we embody this love, we participate in God's saving work in the world: we become the face and voice and hands and feet of Jesus as we wait for him to come again. This is active waiting. And this is what we are to mindfully practice during Advent. True, we should be participating in God's saving work in the world not just during Advent but always. Advent, however, gives us a place to begin, a time when, liturgically, we wait with other Christians, preparing a place for Christ—a place in our hearts, certainly, but also a place in the world. And we do so with joy for, wonder of wonders, our loving God has come!

LIVING THE SEASON

....

The liturgical colors of Advent:
purple (repentance and reflection)
pink (joy)
blue (hope)

During the first week of Advent, consider what connotations the word wait *holds for you. How is "active waiting" similar to your notion of waiting? How is it different? What are ways in which you already engage in active waiting? What are ways you want to deepen or expand the waiting that you do?*

Consider fasting from certain foods, saving your enjoyment of them for Christmas. One family I know fasts from meat during Advent, seeing the weeks between the big feasts of Thanksgiving and Christmas as an appropriate time to embrace a simpler way of eating. Another family fasts from sugar during these weeks before Christmas as a way of practicing waiting. If this seems too difficult (I've tried it—and it is hard!), you could moderate your fast by eating sugar on Sundays (in honor of Christ's resurrection, Sundays are always feast days, that is, days to break one's fast during seasons of fasting) or by choosing two or three kinds of sweets (a favorite cookie, perhaps) to save for Christmas.

Read Malachi 3:1-4 (Old Testament reading for the second Sunday of Advent, year C). What is the significance of the messenger being both one "in whom you delight" and also "a refiner's fire" before whom none can stand? How does this image of the refiner's fire fit with Advent's mood of preparation? What is one thing you would like to do during Advent to prepare your heart for Christ's coming?

Hayley, an at-home mother of two school-age boys, and her family open their stockings on December 6, St. Nicholas Day, an appropriate choice. The origin of the Christmas stocking comes from St. Nicholas, who anonymously dropped a bag of gold coins into the window of a young girl who was without a dowry. According to legend, some of the coins fell into a stocking that was hung up to dry. Thus was born the tradition of stocking stuffing. In addition to opening their stockings, Hayley's family reads stories about St. Nicholas's life. Hayley looks at this as a way of removing Santa Claus from the celebration of Christmas, while not depriving her children of the joy and delight associated with stocking gifts. Consider opening your family's stockings this day.

Read Luke 1:46-55 (canticle, in lieu of the psalm, for the third Sunday of Advent, all years). For those of us in middle-class America (who are among the world's wealthiest people), how is Mary's Magnificat good news? Why do we rejoice with Mary that God "has brought down the powerful from their thrones, | and lifted up the lowly | . . . filled the hungry with good things, | and sent the rich away empty"? How might you engage with and enter into the spirit of Mary's Magnificat during Advent?

Be mindful when you decorate your house for Christmas. Hayley refrains from putting up any Christmas decorations until Christmas Eve and instead decorates her mantle for Advent, draping it with a purple cloth and setting out purple votive candles. My friend Ellie puts up her Christmas decorations slowly, one or two each week. She sees this slow readying of her home for Christmas over the weeks of Advent as a way of mindfully preparing her heart as well as increasing her excitement about and anticipation of Christmas.

2 ∘ *Christmas*

A Season of Celebration

We don't usually have baptisms in December, my pastor told me. I pleaded. My parents would be in town for Christmas, and Doug's parents, who often work weekends, were available to drive down. That convergence of family wouldn't happen again for at least six months, maybe more. My pastor relented. And so Jack was to be baptized on the Sunday after Christmas Day, December 28 that year. At the time I was too distracted by the demands of being a new mother to realize the significance of the date: the Feast of Holy Innocents, the church's commemoration of the children slaughtered by King Herod in his failed attempt to kill the infant Jesus (see Matthew 2:16-18).

The church where I worship does not follow the *Common Lectionary* readings, so on the day of Jack's baptism we did not read Matthew's account of the slaughter of the Innocents. Instead, we continued in our journey through the book of Isaiah, which we had been studying for several months. The passages that day were from Isaiah 24 and 26.

The earth dries up and withers,
    the world languishes and withers;
    the heavens languish together with the earth. . . .
The wine dries up,
    the vine languishes,
    all the merry-hearted sigh.
The mirth of the timbrels is stilled,
    the noise of the jubilant has ceased,
    the mirth of the lyre is stilled.
No longer do they drink wine with singing. . . .
The city of chaos is broken down,
    every house is shut up so that no one can enter. . . .
    all joy has reached its eventide;
    the gladness of the earth is banished.
    (Isaiah 24:4, 7-11)

While my friend Mike read this passage, another friend, Sprague, drew a picture of it on a large chalkboard beside the Communion table. He drew a tree, barren and broken, fire consuming its jagged branches while the earth beneath split open to devour it.

We all sat in stunned silence as the litany of horrors went on, as the flames of fire in Sprague's drawing grew more and more violent and chaotic.

It was a sobering beginning to a baptism. Tears stung my eyes. Is this the world my child has been born into? Did I labor only to bring him into a world of desolation and despair? Where is the joy and peace of Christmas in the midst of this brokenness and pain?

THE ORIGINS OF CHRISTMAS

The celebration of Christ's birth did not become a Christian holy day until the fourth century. Then December 25 was chosen in part because of its connection to pagan solstice celebrations—the idea being, perhaps, that the Feast of the Nativity would give Christians something to celebrate during these raucous pagan festivities or would make Christianity more palatable to pagans. Whatever the pragmatic reasons for choosing this date, the church's choice was also theological and symbolic: how better to embody the mystery of the incarnation than by celebrating the birth of the Word, the Light of the World, the Son of God, in the middle of the darkest time of year?[1] "The light shines in the darkness," the apostle John writes (John 1:5), and so the Feast of the Nativity was appointed for one of the very darkest days of the year.

By the twelfth century, Christmas was the most widely celebrated holy day in Europe. This is reflected by the three masses held on Christmas Day in the Middle Ages. These three masses corresponded to the three births that medieval Christians saw in the Nativity of Christ. The first birth occurred in the Godhead before time began, and so the midnight mass, shrouded in darkness, celebrated the "creative fecundity of the Father" in begetting the Son in eternity.[2] The second mass was at dawn, its morning light mirroring the coming of light into the darkness of the world in the celebration of the "maternal fruitfulness" of Mary as she birthed Jesus, the Son of God, into the world.[3] The third mass, at noon, celebrated the birth of Christ in the souls of each individual Christian through the "fertile indwelling of the Holy Spirit in the hearts and minds of humankind."[4]

In those days, Christmas did not end when midnight struck on December 25, and even today in more liturgical churches, Christmas is a *season* of the church year, its twelve feast days spanning from Christmas Day through Epiphany on January 6.[5] The twelve days of Christmas are among the most joyous of the church year. The liturgical color of these days is white, symbolizing the light of Christ as well as his purity and innocence, and sometimes gold, symbolizing Christ's kingship and triumph over sin and death.

A LONG, SLOW CHRISTMAS

"Midnight on Christmas Eve," writes Wendy Wright, "is the still, silent point of the entire Advent and Christmas season."[6] We are not used to silence. Our lives are encased in sound: the radio, the TV, Muzak in the grocery store, car horns, car engines, ringing cell phones. Throughout December, we are bombarded with Christmas songs wherever we go, whatever radio station we tune in to. Christmas specials fill prime-time TV slots. By the time Christmas Day arrives, many people are sick of Christmas. They just want it to be over with. December is too full of sound and fury, signifying nothing. No wonder people experience post-Christmas blues. One friend of mine says she has to spend all of January recovering from Christmas.

But what if we have been faithful to observe Advent? What if we have been *waiting* with joyful expectation through the weeks of December for the advent of the Christ? What if we have been preparing our hearts to receive the greatest gift humanity has ever been given?

In that case, midnight on Christmas Eve really is the still point when Advent silently turns into Christmas, when our waiting is finally over and the One for whom we have been waiting appears in our midst.

Gathering for a candlelit Communion service on Christmas Eve is one of my favorite childhood memories, and it continues to be one of the most treasured rituals of my year. Walking through the brisk, cold night from the car to the candlelit church, the anticipation is palpable. The dimly lit church is filled with poinsettias—and candles. As we enter the darkened sanctuary, each person is handed a small taper. We listen again to the Christmas story. We sing, at last, the Christmas carols we have been waiting through all of Advent to sing. We receive Communion. We pass the light, the only sound the murmur of soft voices. "Jesus Christ is the Light of the world," we whisper to one another as each person's candle kindles another's until the church is bright with the flames of hundreds of candles. And then, at midnight, we raise our candles high and sing "Joy to the World." It is Christmas! The waiting of Advent is over, and we rejoice: the Lord is come!

When I was a child, my sister and I would leave the church after the Christmas Eve service exuberantly, wild with excitement that Christmas was finally here. It was usually foggy in the middle of the night in California's Central Valley, thick blankets of cold pressing on us as we walked (or rather, my parents walked; my sister and I skipped and hopped and ran) back to our car. Once home, we did not open gifts. Instead, we cuddled up in front of the fireplace and drank hot cocoa before heading to bed.

Though many of my friends would come to the Christmas Eve service having already opened their presents, in my family, the opening of gifts was reserved for Christmas morning. My father's mother had died on Christmas Eve, so the day was a painful one for him. He wanted to honor her memory by refraining from the distraction of opening presents.

Now that I'm grown, I also refrain from opening gifts on Christmas Eve, in part because I grew up that way, but also because my husband's birthday is December 24. I want him to have the chance to celebrate his birthday without it being co-opted by Christmas. So Doug is the only one who gets to open gifts on Christmas Eve, and they're wrapped in birthday paper, not Christmas paper.

Some people have grown up with family traditions of opening one or all presents on Christmas Eve, and this can certainly be meaningful. One family I spoke with chooses to open their Christmas gifts on Christmas Eve because their oldest daughter was born on Christmas Day, and they want her birthday to be a separate celebration from Christmas. She, therefore, is the only one who gets to open presents on her birthday. The challenge for us is to reflect on our practices, as this family has done, and filter them in light of the rhythm of the church calendar.

As Anna, the mother of two college-age sons, said, "There's a lot of tension in observing the church year. You find you're really bucking the culture. And this is more true during Advent and Christmas than any other time of year." She recounts a particularly "disastrous" Christmas morning fifteen years ago, which changed the way she and her family celebrated Christmas: "There were piles and piles of paper and boxes. Everybody was glassy-eyed by 9 a.m. I found myself sitting there in the middle of the chaos, almost in tears, thinking, 'This is awful!'"

From then on, she and her family spread their gift giving over the twelve days of Christmas. "People thought we were nuts, but I found it really diffused the wretched excess of Christmas Day. The guys opened one present each day, and then they could read that book or play with that toy, rather than throwing it aside right away in order to open something else." There were other, unexpected benefits as well, both environmentally and financially: they recycled wrapping paper ("It became a bit of a joke," Anna says, "to see how many times we could use the same piece of wrapping paper"), and they shopped after-Christmas sales for their gifts for the latter days of Christmas.

Hayley, the mother of two school-age boys, also spreads the giving of gifts over the twelve days of Christmas, but she wants the focus of those days to be on Christ rather than on the gifts. To this end, she has purchased twelve ornaments, one for each day of Christmas. Each ornament represents a name of Jesus and has a Scripture passage that corresponds to it. Every evening during Christmas, one of her sons chooses an ornament, hangs it on the Advent wreath that sits in the center of the dining table and reads the Scripture.

In addition, Hayley brings out the Magi for her crèche on Christmas Day, starting them in a back room or the corner of the kitchen. Over the course of the twelve days, the boys move the Magi and their camels ever closer to the manger and the stable, thus preparing them for the culmination of Christmas in the celebration of Epiphany, but also reminding them that Christmas is about seeking—and finding—Jesus.

Christmas—the season, not just the day—is supposed to be a time of joy and celebration, a time to be lingered over and delighted in. If we as the church have been actively waiting through the weeks of Advent for the coming of Christmas, then, unlike our cultural counterparts, we will not be ready to simply toss aside the Christmas season along with the wrapping paper and ribbons on December 26—

and we will not need to. We will have eleven more days to celebrate
with joy what my pastor calls "a long, slow Christmas."

SUFFERING IN THE MIDST OF CELEBRATION

What then of the Innocents? Why recall their suffering in the
middle of this season of joy? Why recall suffering at all? Why not
just eat, drink and be merry?

On the day of Jack's baptism, Isaiah's words hung heavy in
the air: "All joy has reached its eventide; / all gladness of the
earth is banished." Sprague's drawing—the tree engulfed in
flames, falling into the broken earth—held our riveted gazes.
We may not have mentioned the Holy Innocents at my church
that day. We may not have even thought of them. But they were
there, devoured by the sword just as surely as Sprague's tree was
devoured by earth and flame. Herod, prone to power—how it
must have preyed on him—ordered the death of *all* the children,
not just the male children, though he surely knew the girls were
no threat to him. What a horror it was, the slaughter of all those
little ones. How the mothers and fathers must have felt like that
tree, broken down, desolate, helpless, hopeless.

After telling the story of the children's slaughter, Matthew
quotes Jeremiah:

> A voice was heard in Ramah,
>   wailing and loud lamentation,
> Rachel weeping for her children;
>   she refused to be consoled,
>   because they are no more. (Matthew 2:18)

And that is how it feels, on this Holy Innocents day, when we
remember all the children who have died at the hands of despots

and tyrants, be they kings and queens or fathers and mothers. It is a cause for wailing and lamentation.

At first glance it seems odd, out of place, that this commemoration of death, especially the brutal death of the innocent, should fall on the third day of Christmas. Why mar such a joyful season with the appalling remembrance of this horror? But the wisdom of our forebears becomes evident when we pause to consider this question. Fleming Rutledge says, "The Christmas story is anchored to our lives and to the wickedness of this world by the grief of Rachel. . . . The authors of Scripture did not turn away from the unimaginable suffering of children. God the Father did not turn away. Jesus did not turn away."[7] Placing Holy Innocents here, in the midst of Christmas, forces us to face the wickedness of this world, which will intrude on even our most joyful celebrations, showing them to be incomplete, premature.

Similarly, Sprague's drawing seemed to mock us as we muddled through the service, giving our tithes and offerings, praying, singing our praises to God. How to give praise to an almighty God when evil and suffering exist in the world?

Then my friend Steve began to read, and my friend Susan drew on another chalkboard, on the other side of the Communion table.

> On that day, this song will be sung in the land of Judah:
> We have a strong city;
>> [God] sets up victory
>> like walls and bulwarks.
> Open the gates,
>> so that the righteous nation that keeps faith

may enter in.
Those of steadfast mind you keep in peace—
　　in peace because they trust in you.
Trust in the LORD forever,
　　for in the LORD GOD
　　you have an everlasting rock. . . .
Your dead shall live, their corpses shall rise.
　　O dwellers in the dust, awake and sing for joy!
For your dew is a radiant dew,
　　and the earth will give birth to those long dead.
　　(Isaiah 26:1-4, 19)

Susan also drew a tree, but this one was living, its branches, heavy with green leaves and red fruit, reaching to the heavens. It grew on a hilltop, and at its roots was a city, circled by children laughing and dancing.

HOPE FOR OUR FUTURE

During Christmas, we celebrate the truth that Christ, the Light of the world, is with us even in the darkness, and he is the light no darkness can overcome. That is why Holy Innocents needs to be couched within the celebratory season that is Christmas: in grappling with death and evil in the midst of a season of celebration, the celebration itself reminds us that death and evil do not have the last word, just as they did not have the first word. The first word was Christ, and the last word is Christ. Suffering is held within the loving arms of the God who created the cosmos, who became flesh and lived among us, who will one day wipe every tear from our eyes.

In Matthew's account of the Holy Innocents, he ends his quote from Jeremiah with the chilling words "they are no more"

(Jeremiah 31:15). But the passage he is quoting goes on:

> Thus says the LORD:
> Keep your voice from weeping,
>   and your eyes from tears;
> for . . . they shall come back from the land of the enemy;
> there is hope for your future, says the LORD:
>   your children shall come back to their own country.
> (Jeremiah 31:16-17)

Placing Holy Innocents in the midst of the Christmas season reminds us that, in the end, there will be no more death or crying or pain. In the end, the children will be restored to their parents, their siblings, their aunts and uncles and grandparents. In the end, we will be reunited with our lost loved ones. In the end, there will be wholeness and perfect communion. In the end, there will be great rejoicing.

In the meantime, we live with the *hope* of that promise, but not yet its fulfillment. We glimpse the joy of the end in our celebration of Christmas (the season, not simply the day), but we live in the reality of Holy Innocents: bloodshed, violence, separation, heartache. For many in our world, even Christmas is a season of darkness, a time when the loss of loved ones, the reality of loneliness, the pain of estrangement is made all the sharper by its contrast with the prevailing mood of joy that the season engenders in others. Holy Innocents brings that suffering into focus, validating its reality and reminding us that God is present with us in the midst of our pain. Christmas does not ignore pain; it embraces it and transforms it.

Those chalk drawings at the front of the sanctuary on the day of Jack's baptism spoke to the reality of Holy Innocents and also to the reality of Christmas: the dead tree on one side of the Communion table and the baptismal font, the living tree on the other.

How fitting that my son was baptized right in the middle.

For is that not where we all live—between the now and the not-yet of Christ's promise of life? So often our present experience of death and desolation and despair seems overwhelming and more real than the promise of life. But sometimes, thanks be to God, we feel we live in the city of life, where children laugh and sing and dance for joy.

LIVING THE SEASON

The liturgical colors of Christmas:
white (purity, joy)
gold (royalty, triumph)

What is your emotional response to Christmas? Is this a season of celebration for you? A season of sadness? A season that irritates or annoys you? That makes you feel lonely or overwhelmed? Give yourself space to sit in God's presence with whatever you feel, however you respond to this season. Ask what God has for you in the midst of those feelings, in the midst of this season.

On Christmas Day, light the white Christ candle in the center of your Advent wreath to mark the coming of the Light. Continue to light it each evening during Christmas, reciting a simple litany as you do so. Our family uses this one:

Candlelighter: Jesus Christ is the Light of the world.
Everyone else: The Light no darkness can overcome.

If you live alone, you could say the entire litany yourself. A single woman I know lights her Christ candle in the morning as she's getting ready for work, to remind herself that these dark December mornings will not last much longer, that Light will always triumph over darkness.

Read Jeremiah 31:7-14 (Old Testament reading for the second Sunday after Christmas, all years). Where has God acted in this redemptive way in your life, bringing rejoicing and gladness out of a place of brokenness and pain? Where in your life right now do you long for God to lead you "by brooks of water" or to turn your mourning into joy, give you gladness for sorrow?

December 26 is the Feast of St. Stephen, the first martyr. Stephen was a deacon, and one of his duties was to care for the poor in the Jerusalem church. (His feast day became known as Boxing Day in England because of the practice of boxing up charitable gifts on this day.) His faith in Christ led to his being stoned to death. "In our safe American lives," says Hayley, "we don't often think about the cost of following Jesus." And yet here, almost at the beginning of the Christmas season, we have an opportunity to consider that cost. On St. Stephen's Day, volunteer at a local soup kitchen, food bank or homeless shelter, in honor of this deacon who cared for the poor in the Jerusalem church. You could also honor his memory by reading his story in Acts 6–8.

Read Hebrews 2:10-18 (epistle reading for first Sunday after Christmas, year A). According to this passage, why does it matter that Jesus became "perfect through sufferings," that he shared our flesh and blood? How do you respond to this proclamation that Jesus became like us in every respect?

Christmas is a difficult season for many who are far from their families or who have lost loved ones, which makes it especially important to include them in our celebrations. Invite someone for whom Christmas might be a lonely time to join you for a Christmas dinner—not on Christmas Day, but on one of the other twelve days. People often enjoy post–Christmas Day celebrations better simply because they are low-key (compared to the hype and craziness that too often characterize Christmas Day). Extending the celebration in this gentle way can also help alleviate the post-Christmas blues or even depression that so many people experience.

Read John 1:1-14 *(Gospel reading for Christmas Day, all years). Because it is so familiar, this passage sometimes loses its power to amaze us. Read these verses slowly. What strikes you as you read? What might God want to say to you through these well-known words? How do you want to respond to God's gift of Light?*

3 ∘ *Epiphany*

The Gift and the Call

My teddy bear still sits on my bed during the day. Since my wedding, he has slept elsewhere at night, usually on a cozy towel in the armoire in Doug's and my bedroom. Until I got married, except for a long stretch of time that Teddy spent in Spain without me, I had slept with this patchily fuzzy bear nearly every night of my life.

I got Teddy when I was two (hence his stunningly original name, though I decided when I was nine that "Teddy" was short for Theodora Eleanor—never mind that Teddy has always been a *he,* not a *she*). When I was five, I lost him for several days, only to find him sitting on a low table covered with other stuffed animals in my little sister's room. I snatched Teddy off the table and accused my mother, who was tidying it, of stealing him and giving him to Jen, a capital offense if ever there was one.

Teddy came to grade-school sleepovers with me and to summer camp all the way through high school. I took him with me to college, though my whole freshman year I hid him under my bedspread and two pillows, terrified that some mean-spirited prankster would steal him. When I spent a quarter abroad my junior year, Teddy came with me, traveling around the British Isles crammed into my backpack.

Though I sometimes felt embarrassed that I still loved on and slept with a teddy bear, it never occurred to me to put him away. Teddy comforted me when I was sad, danced around the room with me when I was happy, and never interrupted or tried to problem-solve when I needed to pour out my heart.

His solace was especially helpful my first year out of college. I had just finished a harrowing stint as a student teacher and realized that my long-held plan of teaching high school was not something for which I was emotionally cut out. I had no job (and thus no money) and no sense of what sort of work I wanted to do. I had a roommate who was going through a difficult time of her own and was emotionally unavailable, which made me dread being in my apartment. Apart from one dear friend, I had no community. Cuddling with Teddy while I read was among the small handful of things in my life that brought me comfort and a measure of joy.

One day in April of that year, I sat in the lunchroom at one of the many offices at which I temped during those months. As I ate my soup and read from Richard Foster's book *Freedom of Simplicity*, I came upon his suggestion that I, the reader, give up the possession I held most dear. Not *consider* giving it up, but actually *give* it up. I suddenly had a terrifying sense that God was asking me to give Teddy up. My stomach clenched into a knot. I burst into tears, quickly gathered my things and fled the lunchroom in fear and humiliation.

I could not give Teddy up. I would not give Teddy up. The thought of him languishing in a thrift shop and finally being thrown in the garbage made me physically ill. And no one I knew had a child young enough to want a patchy old bear. I wasn't sure such a child existed anyway. Who besides me would love this tattered stuffed animal? Still, the nagging sense that I was supposed to give Teddy up remained.

A year later, I had gainful employment, a church community, a boyfriend who adored me and a delightful cat who slept on my feet at night. The cat would have liked to sleep on my chest, but Teddy still occupied that spot. I was happier, less lonely and less broke than I had been the year before. My primary sadness was that my best friend was moving to Spain.

And that's when it dawned on me: I would send Teddy to Spain with Christa. Having never been without Teddy for more than a night or two, I trembled a little when I handed her the wrapped parcel, but mostly I felt joy and gladness at being able to give my beloved friend a meaningful gift. Christa knew how much Teddy meant to me. She understood that in sending Teddy with her to Spain, I was giving her part of myself.

My giving of my teddy bear to Christa gave me an experiential glimpse of the very heart of Christianity. I had always thought Jesus had given up equality with God and emptied himself, taking human form, out of a sense of martyred obligation: as if he were a divine Eeyore, sighing over our sorry state and saying, "Well, somebody's got to fix this mess, and I guess it's up to me." But that's not true: in Christ, God gave himself to us, not because he had to but because he wanted to, because he loved us. Like (in an admittedly small way) my giving of Teddy, Christ's coming was a sacrifice, to be sure, but it was also a joy. Indeed, the joy far outweighed the sacrifice.

On Epiphany, that is what we celebrate: the good news of the coming of God the Son for the whole earth, an extravagant gift of joy-filled love.

THE ORIGINS OF EPIPHANY

Just as Advent culminates in Christmas, Christmas culminates in Epiphany, which means "manifestation" or "showing forth." In the early centuries of Christianity, Epiphany was (with Easter and Pentecost) one of the three major Christian feasts, the celebration of both Christ's birth and his baptism. The Eastern church, which calls this holy day Theophany, "divine manifestation," continues this tradition. In the Western church, beginning in the fourth century, the birth of Christ gradually became separated from his baptism (which is now observed on the Sunday following Epiphany), and Epiphany came to be associated with the coming of the Magi, that is, with the appearance of Christ to the Gentiles.

The story of the Magi is told in Matthew 2. Though the identity of the Magi remains mysterious, they were likely members of a "respected class of scholars who devoted themselves to the study of natural sciences, medicine, mathematics, astronomy, and astrology."[1] Contrary to our popular imagination, they were probably not kings. That idea came about over the next few hundred years, as Christians read passages like Isaiah 60 and saw in these prophetic words a foretelling of the Magi's visit:

Arise, shine; for your light has come,
   and the glory of the Lord has risen upon you. . . .
Nations shall come to your light,
   and *kings* to the brightness of your dawn. . . .
[T]he wealth of the nations shall come to you.
A multitude of camels shall cover you,

> the young camels of Midian and Ephah;
> all those from Sheba shall come.
> They shall bring gold and frankincense,
> and shall proclaim the praise of the LORD.
> (Isaiah 60:1, 3, 5-6, emphasis mine)

Early Christians read their knowledge of the Christ-story back into these words. They saw Jesus as the light who has come, and the Magi as the kings who come to the brightness of the dawning Christ-light, bringing their gifts of gold and frankincense. (Matthew includes myrrh among their gifts.) From this passage, too, comes the inclusion of camels in our imagining of the Magi's visit.

In the eighth century, the Venerable Bede, an English historian, recorded embellishments of Matthew's account of the Magi, including the names of the "Three Kings" and their physical descriptions: Melchior was old, white-haired and brought gold; Caspar was a ruddy young man bearing frankincense; and Baltasar was a heavily bearded, dark-skinned man who brought myrrh.

Whether the Magi were kings or astrologers, the material fact is that they were Gentiles—pagans—and as such represent all non-Jewish peoples. When these pagans saw the star, they left all they had and knew to follow it, for they recognized it as the sign of the Messiah, "not only for the 'religious' people (the Jews), but for the heathen Gentiles (that's us) as well. . . . They recognized Jesus Christ as the one to whom they owed their ultimate allegiance."[2] In the coming of the Magi, God's covenantal relationship with Israel, "fulfilled in Jesus, becomes available to all people."[3]

THE GIFT OF THE MAGI

Two interrelated themes emerge from the story of the Magi.[4] The first is gift-giving. The tradition of gift-giving on Christmas originated because of the gifts the Magi brought to the Christ child—recall that for the first few centuries of Christianity, Christmas and Epiphany were celebrated the same day. Over the centuries, the gift-giving shifted to become a practice of expressing affection or of responding to needs—like St. Nicholas's gift of gold for a poor girl's dowry—until in our own day, it has become a "veritable orgy of conspicuous consumption,"[5] devouring the entire month of December.

But it need not be so. Indeed, it ought not be so.

Part of the problem with our current conception of gift-giving is that too often it is merely about giving stuff, things, experiences, rather than giving ourselves. Now, things can certainly be gifts of self, but it is increasingly rare in our affluent society that an object will capture the sacrificial nature that gift-giving requires in order for it to be meaningful. A lovely example of this kind of giving is found in O. Henry's short story "The Gift of the Magi," in which Jim and Della, a poor young couple, each give up their greatest treasure in order to buy a Christmas gift for the other. Jim's treasure is his grandfather's exquisite gold pocket watch. Della's is her hair, which when unbound falls nearly to her knees, like a mantle. Having scrimped and saved for months, Della has still only managed to save $1.87 for Jim's gift, so she sells her hair for twenty dollars and with the money buys him a beautifully simple platinum fob for his watch. When Jim comes home, he sees her shorn head and, in stupefaction, gives her the present he bought for her—a set of beautiful tortoise-shell combs for her hair—a gift he purchased by selling his watch. Jim and Della gave each other things, to be sure, but the physical gifts were meaningful because of the great sacrifice of love that made them possible.

Another example of such sacrificial giving occurs in John 12, when Mary of Bethany pours nard on the feet of Jesus and wipes them with her hair. I confess that I am too much like Judas Iscariot, who snipes about the wastefulness of Mary's gift to Jesus: "Why was this perfume not sold? Why was the money not given to the poor?" Why, indeed? Yet Jesus defends Mary, telling Judas to leave her alone, commending her foresight in anointing his body for burial (see John 12:1-8). We can judge Mary to be profligate and a poor steward of her financial resources, but in doing so, we align ourselves not with Jesus, but with Judas, his betrayer, the one who had already shut out love.

I once heard a sermon on this passage in which the preacher tried to give the congregation a modern-day example of the extravagance of Mary's gift. He told this little parable: Imagine that all his adult life, your best friend has been a huge U2 fan. Their music has shaped his life and lives close to his heart. Now imagine that he is dying. Before he dies, he wants to see U2 play in concert again. His birthday, likely his last, is approaching. You want to take him to a U2 concert—you'll pay for his ticket and his airfare to get there—but he is too ill to travel. So you hire U2 to come and play a private concert for this U2-loving best friend's birthday party. To finance this extravagant gift, you spend all your savings—for next year's vacation, for a house, for your retirement. You max out all your credit cards. You sell your car.[6]

That's a pretty good approximation. After all, Mary wasn't wealthy. This nard, worth a year's wages, was probably her dowry. Using it to anoint Jesus' feet meant she would never have the means to marry, which meant that she would likely not have the means to live—a single woman in that culture did not have a lot of options. Even knowing this, she poured out her extravagant gift in an outpouring of love. "Love," says William Barclay, "is not love if it nicely calculates the cost."[7]

What Epiphany calls us to is this sort of extravagant giving, with great love, without counting the cost, the sort of giving that I did when I gave my beloved teddy bear to my beloved friend; the sort of giving that Della and Jim did, giving up their only treasures to buy a gift worthy of the other; the sort of giving Mary did when she spent her greatest possession on Jesus.

Our culture is cynical about such giving, believing it to be foolish, even outright stupid. But beneath the cynicism is, I think, deep longing. We want others to give us the gift of themselves. We want to give the gift of ourselves. We want to know and be known. We want to love deeply and be loved in return. The good news of Epiphany is that we are. God knows us and longs for us to know him, which is why he became flesh and dwelt among us, why he sent the star to the Magi. God wanted all the world to know him and experience his love.

FOLLOW THAT STAR

The second theme that Epiphany raises is of call and response. The wise men saw the star and so they left all that was familiar and dear to follow it, knowing it would lead them to something even better. Traditionally on Epiphany, people bless their homes by marking the lintel of their door in chalk with the initials *C, M* and *B.* The initials have two meanings. They are the names of the three wise men, according to tradition— Caspar, Melchior and Baltasar—and they are the first letters of the Latin phrase *Christus Mansionem Benedicat* ("Christ, bless this home"). Marking the door of one's home in this way is a reminder to us, each time we enter or leave, that we are to be like the wise men, willing to leave all we have, if necessary, to follow where Christ leads.

Raised in a church culture that viewed suffering and even martyrdom for the sake of God's kingdom as signs of true faith, I have a lot of baggage around this notion of leaving it all to follow Jesus. A dear friend of mine perfectly articulated the deleterious effect of the evangelical mindset in which I was raised when she wailed, "But I'm afraid to follow Jesus. I don't want to go to Africa!" I could relate. I used to be afraid of that too, of Jesus asking me to follow him to some faraway place with giant spiders. I had learned early and well that you proved your devotion to Jesus by the sacrifices you were willing to make on his behalf.

This is partly why, when I was in eighth grade, I chose Mother Teresa as the subject of a yearlong research project for a national competition. Mother Teresa obviously loved Jesus; her life of (what seemed to me) great sacrifice was clear evidence of her devotion. I wanted to know how she did it.

As part of my research, my teacher insisted that I call Mother Teresa. Now, I was seventeen before I could phone Pizza Hut and order a pizza without breaking into a cold sweat, so imagine my terror when, at thirteen, I had to call India and speak to Mother Teresa. "Why couldn't I have chosen to research someone dead?" I moaned more than once as this horror loomed over me.

At last I could put it off no longer. My list of questions on my lap, I shut myself in my bedroom and made the call. My voice shook and my hands trembled as I lamely introduced myself and then idiotically launched into my questions. "What advice would you have for someone who wants to help the poor?" I squeaked into the phone.

I expected some great thing: come to India and join the Missionaries of Charity, work in the House of the Dying, adopt sixteen orphan children. Instead, her voice quavery, her accent difficult to understand, Mother Teresa said, "Love the poor around you. Learn to see the poverty in the people you live with, and love them in the midst of it." That's all she said. For years, I thought it too simple, too easy, too pat. Love those around you? That's it? That's how I love the poor of the world? I had been thoroughly indoctrinated with the good-Christians-go-to-Africa-and-die-of-poisonous-spider-bites worldview.

Lately, though, I've begun to see that loving those around me isn't simple. Nor is it easy. It's not easy, for example, to love my son when he whines and won't eat the dinner I've prepared. It's not easy to love my daughter when she throws a temper tantrum because I won't let her eat a Lego. Some days, believe me, the poor of Calcutta seem like a lot better deal. But that's not where I've been called, not yet anyway.

For most of us, following the star means paying attention to the people around us, our families, friends, neighbors. Christ calls us to minister to them. If we don't heed that call, what makes us think we'll really be able to love and care for our Indian neighbors once we move into the House of the Dying?

Epiphany calls us to move beyond the familiar, to be sure. But sometimes, maybe even most of the time, the familiar is not geographical. It may be the familiarity of something we own and hold dear, as it was for me when God called me to let go of Teddy. It may be the familiarity of an unhealthy relationship; the strained and fruitless ways we try to reach out to God; the soul-eroding habits that keep us from loving God and others as we ought; or a familiar pattern of relating or responding to others that Jesus is calling us to set aside that we might follow him.

Perhaps these days I am called to leave behind my usual response of raising my voice and barking orders at Jack when he whines about his dinner. Perhaps Jesus is inviting me to quit throwing my arms up in frustration at Jane when she wails because I won't let her choke on Legos. Perhaps, instead, I'm supposed to give them a hug, extend my arms—and my heart—toward them with love.

After all, isn't that what God did for us?

LIVING THE SEASON

The liturgical color of Epiphany:
white (purity, joy)

Read Isaiah 60:1-6 (Old Testament reading for Epiphany, all years). What are the gifts the nations and kings bring? What are the gifts God gives? How do the gifts of the kings (and by extension, our own gifts) mirror or point to the gifts of God?

Take down your Christmas tree, and put away your Christmas decorations. (It's easier to wait till January 6 to take them down if they haven't been up since Thanksgiving!) Anna's family loved their tradition of taking down the tree on Epiphany. "It felt like Christmas had an official end," Anna says. "Culturally, Christmas just disappears after the twenty-fifth, so this gave us a sense of intentionality about its ending."

Read Ephesians 3:1-12 (epistle reading for Epiphany, all years). What is the significance of Paul's message of the "boundless riches of Christ" for the Gentiles? Who are the "gentiles" of our day? Who are the gentiles in your life? What is God's call to you in relation to them?

Host a house blessing. Traditionally Epiphany has been a day to bless the house or apartment you live in by marking the lintel of your main door in chalk with the inscription 20 C+M+B 09 (or 10 if it's 2010, and so forth). First comes the blessing of the chalk that you will use to make the inscription:

> Lord Jesus Christ, make holy with Your blessing this simple creature, chalk. Make it, for this Epiphany occasion, a special marker for us, who use it with faith and inscribe

with it upon the entrance of our home. May this inscription remind all who enter and leave this house/apartment throughout the year to seek Your light as they journey forth to the wider world of work and play. This we ask in Your holy name. Amen.

Following the blessing of the chalk is the house blessing. You could do this in a number of ways, one person marking the door while another prays, or praying first and then marking the door.

Lord God of Heaven and Earth, You revealed Your only-begotten Son to every nation by the light of a star. Bless this house and all who inhabit it. Allow us to find it a shelter of peace and health. Make our house a place of warmth and caring for all who visit us. Fill us with the light of Christ, that we might clearly see You in our work and play. We ask this through Christ our Lord. Amen.[8]

Traditionally this inscription is left up all year (though it will fade until it is all but invisible, especially if your door is exposed to the elements). Whenever you enter or leave the house, seeing the inscription could remind you to pray that you, like the Magi, might be ready to follow Christ wherever he leads you, in ways both large and small.

Read Matthew 2:1-12 (Gospel reading for Epiphany, all years). The Magi were "overwhelmed with joy" when they saw Jesus. What in your life has evoked a similar response? What hope or dream are you pursuing with the zeal of the Magi? Where do you sense God's call to "follow the star"?

4 ∘ Ordinary Time

The Presentation of Jesus

In January 2007 the *Washington Post* conducted an experiment. For forty-three minutes during morning rush hour inside a Washington, D.C., Metro station, internationally acclaimed violinist Joshua Bell, clad in jeans and a long-sleeved T-shirt, played some of the world's greatest classical music on his Stradivarius. The *Post* expected to have problems with crowd control. But of the almost 1,100 people who walked past Bell that morning, only one person recognized him and only four stopped to listen to him for any length of time. The rest passed by, either not noticing or not caring.

When I heard this story, and then read it for myself, my first thought was, *That figures.* In a culture as busy, hurried and preoccupied as ours, it is hardly surprising that we think we don't have time to stop and listen to a street performer, even an amazing one. Our schedules and to-do lists are so full that we don't have time for disruptions, even beautiful ones.

Many of the people who passed Bell that morning didn't even notice that he was there. In fact, the only people who consistently noticed him and stopped to listen—or tried to—were children. In every case, their parents hurried them along. I like to think that if my kids and I had been in the Metro station that morning, I would have let Jack and Jane stop and listen. I like to think we would have stayed for the whole concert.

But I'm deluding myself. After all, until reading this article, I'd never heard of Joshua Bell. Would I really stop during rush hour to listen to a random violinist, even if he was fabulously good? If I had nowhere to go, maybe. But during rush hour, when I needed to be at work or a meeting or someplace people were expecting me, waiting for me? Not a chance. Like those thousand-some other people, I would have walked right on by, missing this amazing concert, given free, by one of the world's greatest violinists.

It strikes me that this story is a good image for Ordinary Time. In the midst of our daily lives, it is all too easy to get ground down by our tasks and responsibilities until we become blind and deaf to all but the routine busyness of our lives. But when we are too busy, too hurried or too preoccupied with our work, our schedules, our agendas, we miss out on the ways and places God encounters us—or tries to—in the midst of, say, rush hour on an ordinary Friday morning. We don't give ourselves time or permission to notice, let alone stop and listen awhile. Living the season of Ordinary Time can hallow our daily lives and enable us to remember that God is with us—always and everywhere.

THE WISDOM OF ORDINARY TIME

A season of Ordinary Time follows each of the tripartite cycles of the church year: Advent/Christmas/Epiphany and Lent/Easter/ Pentecost. The weeks between Epiphany and Ash Wednesday thus comprise the first cycle of Ordinary Time.

The weeks of Ordinary Time encompass well over half the year (thirty-three or thirty-four Sundays, depending on the date of Easter and on what day of the week Christmas Day falls), which means we live out the bulk of our lives in this season. This seems appropriate, for Ordinary Time is the daily, repetitive—even dull—place where we live most of the time.

The word *ordinary* is rooted in the word *ordinal,* to count. Thus, these "days between," as writer Wendy Wright calls them, are not simply ordinary in the way we usually use that word— uneventful, unimportant, boring—but are actually "Counted Time," time that counts, that matters.[1]

Designating the bulk of each liturgical year as "Ordinary Time" is a profound way of recognizing that the daily, ordinary rhythms of our lives are sacred; that there is something holy to be found in the midst of what often feels like the daily grind; that God is just as present in the grittiness (and the glory) of an ordinary day as in the great celebrations of Christmas or Easter or Pentecost.

The promise of Ordinary Time is that God is present in the midst of such daily activities as my interactions with my husband and children, with my friends and neighbors; in my caring for the needs of my body; in my work for the day, whether it be writing a book or sweeping a floor. Because God is present and active in the midst of the very tasks that often seem pointless, these tasks can, if I'm paying attention, become means of grace—and of growth in my relationship with God. It is fitting, therefore, that the liturgical color of Ordinary Time is green, the color of growth.

THE PRESENTATION OF JESUS

The Feast of the Presentation of our Lord falls on February 2, in the first cycle of Ordinary Time, and speaks of the importance of attentiveness in the midst of our ordinary lives. This feast is celebrated forty days after Christmas. According to the Gospel of Luke, Mary and Joseph took Jesus to be presented in the temple forty days after his birth, in conjunction with Mary's rite of purification after childbirth.[2]

The Feast of the Presentation is also called Candlemas. On February 2, Kathleen Norris, spending a year at St. John's Abbey in central Minnesota, writes,

> Today, the monks are doing something that seems futile, and a bit foolish. They are blessing candles, all the candles they'll use during worship for the coming year. It's good to think of the light hidden inside those new candles; walking to prayer each morning in the bitter cold, I know that the light comes earlier now. I can feel the change, the hours of daylight increasing.[3]

The connection between the story of Jesus' presentation in the temple and the blessing of candles comes from Simeon's song in Luke 2. God had promised Simeon he would live to see the Messiah. Prompted by the Holy Spirit, Simeon goes to the temple just as Mary and Joseph are bringing Jesus in. Taking the infant in his arms, Simeon proclaims him a light to reveal God to the nations and the glory of Israel (see Luke 2:32).

Simeon's reference to Jesus as the light that reveals God to the nations prompted the connection to Christ our Light, which is represented symbolically during the liturgy throughout the year in the lighting of candles. In the Western church, the annual blessing of those candles began sometime in the Middle Ages, possibly as a way of Christianizing pagan midwinter lambing rituals as Christianity spread north and west into Europe.

Whatever its origins, the ritual blessing of the candles fits this feast day theologically and liturgically. It continues the imagery of light begun in Advent, a theme that culminates in the coming of the Light in the celebration of the incarnation at Christmas. That Light is made manifest to the whole world in the coming of the Magi, who follow the light of the star to find the new King. Simeon confirms this revelation of the light to the Gentiles and further declares Jesus the glory of Israel.

Simeon's proclamation is echoed in the psalm for the day, which heralds Jesus the "King of glory" coming in strength and might to the temple (Psalm 24:10). So glorious is this king that even the gates of Jerusalem rise up to join the celebration. Thus, as early as the late 300s, this feast day was honored with a procession to the Basilica of the Resurrection in Jerusalem, followed by a joyful mass, in which the Gospel passage was the story of Simeon's and Anna's encounters with Jesus in the temple.

Simeon's life is a beautiful picture of faithfulness. Day in, day out, through the ordinary rituals and rhythms of his days, he waited, eager for the consolation of Israel, attentive to the Holy Spirit, wondering when he would see the promised Messiah. I wonder if he ever grew tired of waiting. I wonder if he ever forgot to pay attention. I wonder if he sometimes even forgot what he was waiting for. But on this day, at least, the day of Jesus' presentation, he is paying attention. He hears the Spirit prompting him to go to the temple. Ascending the hill of the Lord and entering the temple, the righteous Simeon sees the infant Jesus.

Though the Bible does not record Simeon's initial response, I can't help but think he might have been a little surprised when the Holy Spirit said, "Over there, see that baby? That's the Messiah." I imagine Simeon was expecting someone a little older, someone

stronger, someone more impressive. But Simeon, on whom the
Holy Spirit rests, knows he has heard God correctly. He takes the
baby Jesus in his arms and knows him for the Savior of the world.
God's word to Simeon has been fulfilled.

Anna is a prophet, someone who hears God's word and speaks
it to the people. Though she is old (eighty-four, Luke tells us), she
lives at the temple, worshiping there "with prayer and fasting
night and day" (Luke 2:37). Like Simeon, she sees the child and
immediately knows he is the Messiah. Fulfilling her prophetic
calling, she acclaims Jesus as Redeemer to all who are "looking
for the redemption of Jerusalem" (verse 38). For Anna, this day
starts as just another day at the temple, a day of prayer and fasting
like all the days that had gone before it. And yet, it is *the* day, the
day she meets her Redeemer in the flesh, in the tiny body of a six-
week-old baby. Her long years of waiting and fasting and praying
had brought her to this moment: the light of the world flares
brightly in her eyes, and she beholds his glory.

PAYING ATTENTION

I want to be like Simeon and Anna: attentive to the prompting
of the Holy Spirit; waiting with patient, joyful expectation that I
will indeed see God; and so present to the holy wonder of God-
with-us that I, too, recognize Jesus when he comes, however
odd his appearance may be. In writing that, I have to laugh at
myself because I'm so far from being that person, it's downright
ridiculous. I have moments of mindful attention to the moment
at hand, but mostly I'm like those people in the Metro, rushing
to work and missing the Joshua Bell concert. Most of the time, I
rush headlong through my life and don't even notice that God
is there, trying to surprise me with beauty and joy and light in

unexpected places. This is particularly true during the long weeks of Ordinary Time, when there are no seasons of preparation or celebration to catch my attention and focus it on Jesus.

Thus, during Ordinary Time, I find it especially needful to embrace the spiritual disciplines of *lectio divina* and a daily examen, to help me stop and look at my life, to notice it and also to notice the ways God is present in it.

Now, I read the lectionary each day—at least, I try to—but reading is usually about all I manage, since I'm often trying to squeeze it in between, say, changing my daughter's diaper and rushing off to my son's piano lesson. *Lectio divina,* which is Latin for "holy reading," requires more of my interaction with Scripture than merely "squeezing it in." The latter is preferable to not reading it at all, of course, but *lectio* invites me to actually sit with the Scriptures for a while, to ponder them and my response to them, to listen to what God might be saying to me through them. For now, this requires a level of space and quiet that I, with my two young children scampering about, simply don't get on a daily basis.

Instead I have my *lectio* passages posted on note cards in various strategically located places around the house—by the front door, on the cupboard above the stove, next to my closet and bedroom doors. These remind me to pause, to breathe, to hear the word of the Lord. I might not be able to sit in silence for twenty minutes a day and savor the Scriptures in a traditional *lectio* format, but I can still ponder God's Word in my heart as I go about the tasks and errands of my day. I can still let God's Word comfort me, convict me or even pierce me. I can stand still for a moment, in interior silence, before God's Word.

At the close of each day, I try to spend a few moments reflecting on the day's events and on my responses, noticing those places where I sensed God's presence and also those places where I didn't, what is called an examen. I've been practicing the examen off and on for eight years now, and I've found that the more regularly I practice it, the more I become overwhelmed by a sense of God's goodness and grace to me. It springs up not just in my reflections at the end of the day, but during the day as well—a sudden sense of God being near, of an accident averted, of the sheer beauty of life. I've found that a daily examen helps me pay attention, not just in the act of looking back, but in the moment. It helps me see that even on hard days or during hard seasons, God is present, that though God's grace may not feel like it's abounding in those difficult times, it is sufficient. And the examen helps me remember those graced moments, perhaps because it helps me notice them in the first place.

THE EARTHWORM

While the residents of Washington, D.C., were rushing past Joshua Bell on that Friday morning, I was in Hawaii. The ten days we spent on Maui were glorious. Each day seemed longer than it would have been at home. I moved more slowly, more mindfully than I usually do, aware that my time in this beautiful place was limited and wanting to savor each moment. I watched the water crash against the rocks outside our condo. I watched Doug teach Jack how to swim, while I sat on the shore with Jane and let the warm waves gently lap over our feet and legs. I watched humpback whales breach alongside our boat when we went snorkeling. And I sensed the presence of God in each of these moments.

Then I went home, and the busyness that is my life engulfed me once again. I didn't want it to be that way. But feeling overwhelmed by the minutiae of daily life is almost a habitual response for me. I react to this sense of too much to do and too little time to do it by hurrying, by trying to get some of the things on my to-do list checked off. If I stop rushing around for a moment and just breathe, I realize that all those things I "have" to do aren't really that important. Do I really have to clean the bathroom and sweep the floors and make my kids lunch and put the clothes in the dryer and check email and return a phone call and plan a liturgy and play Legos *right now?* Of course not.

Only one thing is needful in any given moment, and that one thing is prayer, a grateful awareness of the presence of God in *this* moment. With that realization firmly in my mind and heart, the sense of urgency with which I approach my life falls away, and I can discern which of the many things that need doing is the thing that needs doing *right now.* The problem is, I have to stop to remember this. And I am usually too busy rushing to remember to stop! I need help to stop, reminders to draw me up short in my tracks. My *lectio* cards help me stop. The examen helps me stop. Our ten days in Hawaii helped me stop. And a few weeks later, an earthworm helped me stop.

Jack and I were walking home from the park one cold, sunny morning in early February. (It might even have been February 2.) As usual, I was walking faster than my son, who tends to be a dawdler, and was a half-dozen paces ahead of him when he called out, "Mama!"

I turned.

"Mama, look!" Jack was crouching on the ground, watching something on the sidewalk. I walked back toward him. An earthworm was making its arduous way from someone's lawn to the grass of the planting strip. Jack stared at it in rapt attention.

Ordinarily I would have snapped at him to leave the worm alone, to hurry up because we needed to get home. But something in me paused; a still, small voice reminded me, kindly, "You say you want to move slowly, to be mindful. Why don't you try it?"

So I stopped and looked, as Jack had so eagerly commanded me to. Jane was asleep in the frontpack I wore, so the only reason we needed to get home was for lunch. Since Jack was obviously more interested in the worm than in lunch at the moment, I crouched down too, and together we watched the worm slither across the sidewalk and burrow into the grass once it reached the planting strip.

In those few moments, I was like Simeon and Anna, attentive to the presence of God in the moment at hand. I was the person I want to be always, filled with joy and wonder at the goodness and beauty of God and this world he made. I pray for more such moments, every day.

LIVING THE SEASON

....

The liturgical color of Ordinary Time:

green (growth)

When you sit down for a meal at home, light a green candle. In our family, we continue to use the Christmas litany throughout this cycle of Ordinary Time.

Candlelighter: Jesus Christ is the light of the world.
Everyone else: The light no darkness can overcome!

Each time you light the candle, let it remind you that God is present and active even in the most ordinary and unremarkable moments of your life. Perhaps even stop for a moment and give God thanks for his presence with you, whether you sense God or not.

Read Luke 2:22-40 (Gospel passage for the Feast of the Presentation, all years). Simeon's words in verses 29 to 32 are called the Nunc dimittis *and are part of the Compline (Close of the Day) service of the Liturgy of the Hours. Why might Christians have chosen these words to pray right before retiring for the night? What effect do these words have on you as you ponder them?*

If you do not already have a daily practice of Bible reading, consider using the daily lectionary. For each day, there are two morning psalms and two evening psalms; an Old Testament reading; a reading from the Epistles, Acts or Revelation; and a Gospel passage. Following the daily readings, you will read through the Bible every two years. You can find the daily lectionary passages in most mainline denominational prayer books (the Anglican

Book of Common Prayer, for example, or the Presbyterian Book of Common Worship). You can also find the passages online by doing an Internet search of "daily lectionary."

Read Hebrews 2:14-18 (epistle reading for the Feast of the Presentation, all years). How might this passage, particularly verse 18, help you to focus your attention on Christ and notice the ways he is present in your life?

Practice a daily examen. A centuries-old Christian discipline, the examen seems especially apropos for Ordinary Time because it helps us become aware of God's presence with us and also aware of our inattention to God. Traditionally done at the close of the day, the examen could also be done weekly, monthly or yearly, though its fruits are most clearly seen when it is practiced on a daily basis.

Here's a brief introduction to the practice. Sit down in a comfortable position, preferably with your feet on the floor and your back straight. Close your eyes and take a moment to center yourself. You might want to take several long, deep breaths. If you have a breath prayer (see chapter eight), now would be a great time to pray it. If not, simply imagine that you are inhaling the presence of God and exhaling all the exhaustion and busyness of the day.

When your breathing is slow and steady, gently review the events of the day, asking God to bring to your attention a time or place during the day when you sensed his presence. This can take any number of forms: a felt sense of joy or delight or of being loved; a moment of mindful attention to God; a meaningful or loving interaction with another person; an encounter with the created world. Whatever it is (and that list is just a smattering of examples), simply notice it and give God thanks for that moment.

Next, ask God to bring to mind a time or place when you were *not* aware of his presence. Again, this can take many forms: a felt sense of sadness or rejection; a lost opportunity to show love or hospitality to another person; a harsh word spoken or heard. Whatever it is, simply notice it. If it is something for which you need to ask God's forgiveness, do so, then rest assured in his pardon. If it is something for which you do not need to ask forgiveness, simply sit with it in God's presence.

Close by praying a breath prayer, the Lord's Prayer or another prayer. Over time, the examen helps us to become more aware, moment by moment, of the work and presence of God in the daily, ordinary moments of our lives.

5 ∘ Lent

A Season of Darkness

Doug came home from Morning Prayer with a black smudge on his forehead. I started to tell him so and to reach up to wipe it off when I realized what it was: the sign of the cross in ashes. Today was Ash Wednesday, the first day of the liturgical season known as Lent. I usually attend an evening service on Ash Wednesday, so the thought of Doug's going to work—going out into the world—with an ashen cross on his forehead gave me pause. What would people think? What, if anything, would they say? For of course they would notice. You couldn't help but notice. The mark was unmistakable.

Still, I resisted the urge to suggest Doug wipe it off. After all, we are but dust and to dust we shall return, and we so seldom stop long enough to even consider this fact of our existence, let alone dwell with it for a while. And so I kept silent, and Doug left for work, marked with an ashen cross. Perhaps that mark would be a witness to the stark reality of our mortality and the hope we have in Christ.

That evening, Doug and I went together to our church and went forward to receive the imposition of ashes. I was standing behind a young man holding his sleeping infant son in his arms. The pastor marked the father's forehead. "Remember that you are dust, and to dust you will return." Then he marked the son's forehead, and my eyes stung with tears. "You are dust," he whispered to the sleeping baby, "and to dust you will return."

As the pastor marked my forehead with ashes in the sign of a cross and solemnly proclaimed my mortality, I wept and wondered achingly why Doug and I had wanted children, why we think it not just morally acceptable but actually *good* to bring them into this world, out of which there is but one way: the way of death.

From receiving the imposition of ashes, I moved to the side of the sanctuary, where two of my friends stood holding a plate of bread and a chalice, the body and blood of Jesus, to be reminded that death does not have the last word.

You see, the whole season of Lent is compressed in this Ash Wednesday service: the painful acknowledgment of my mortality, the sense of sadness at the reality of having to let go of all I hold dear, the proclamation of Jesus' death on my behalf and thus the hope of resurrection.

But that resurrection hope is not yet realized. Lent has begun, and I need—we all need—to live in this space, this dark place between the ashes and the bread and wine, between the declaration of our mortality and the declaration of Christ's redeeming work on our behalf. That is what Lent is, a time to reckon with the reality of darkness and death. We do so with hope, because this season of darkness ends in Easter, in resurrection, in new life. But we can be raised to new life only if we have first died to the old one. That is the challenge—and the gift—of Lent.

THE ORIGINS OF LENT

It is appropriate that Lent begins with this ashen cross marked on our flesh, for from its earliest days, Lent has been a season of dying, of giving up, of clearing out, of emptying. It originated in the early years of the church as a forty-hour fast from Good Friday to Easter Sunday, mirroring the time Christ was in the grave. By the end of the fourth century, the forty hours had evolved into a forty-day period stretching from Ash Wednesday to Easter (not counting Sundays, which are always feast days), and the fast as an expression of sorrow over Christ's death gradually shifted to become an expression of sorrow over the *cause* of Christ's death: our sin. The forty days of Lent were meant to be a reminder of the forty days of rain during the flood, in which God purified the world; the forty years of wilderness wandering, in which God purified Israel; and the forty days of Jesus' fasting in the desert in preparation for his ministry.

In addition to fasting, traditional Lenten observances include repentance and almsgiving, an archaic term in whose place we would probably use the word *charity*. It strikes me that these disciplines of repentance and almsgiving are made possible by the Lenten fast. Fasting opens up space in our lives for us to listen to God, which often leads to repentance. In the Bible, too, especially the Old Testament, fasting is often linked to repentance and to concern for the poor and oppressed.

FASTING

Given that Lent evolved from a pre-Easter fast, it is not surprising that fasting is the practice most commonly associated with this season. My introduction to Lent was through the practice of fasting. In high school, my Catholic friends would talk about what they were giving up for Lent. Being of an ascetical bent, even at age sixteen, this idea of depriving myself of something was appealing. I think my first Lenten fast was from chocolate. I didn't understand *why* I was giving up chocolate. It seemed to me to be enough that I was willing to deny myself: surely that signified my desire to please God and was bound to earn his favor.

Each year, my fasts became more and more extreme. For a couple of years I fasted from all food on Wednesdays and Fridays, which are traditional fast days—Wednesdays commemorate Ash Wednesday and Fridays recall Good Friday, the day Jesus was crucified. One year I gave up all food for Holy Week (the week before Easter) and drank only water. When I collapsed in my fencing class halfway through the week, I began to drink herbal teas and juice, and felt myself a spiritual weakling and a disappointment to God. In all this fasting, my focus was on the "self" in self-deprivation and self-denial. I was wholly absorbed with myself and what *I* was doing to please God, and the more burdensome the fast, the more I thought I must be pleasing God.

In recent years, my understanding of the purpose of the Lenten fast has undergone a gradual but radical change. I have come to see that my "sacrifice" during Lent is not somehow going to earn God's favor or make me more acceptable to God. (Indeed, considering that Lent is a prelude to Christ's death—the ultimate expression of God's grace—it strikes me as incredibly ironic that I ever thought I could *earn* God's favor by fasting during Lent.) As long as those were my aims, I was missing the point. For the point of Lent isn't what I give up, or even if I give anything up. The point is that I am intentionally creating space in my life for my relationship with God.

Fasting, when done with proper motives, is an amazingly fruitful way to create that space, for it creates in us an emptiness—where there used to be something (food, a book, a TV show), now there is a blank, a hole, a space. God longs for those blank, empty places in our lives—not for the sake of emptiness, but so God can fill us with himself. If our bodies are too full of food or our lives too full of activity, we have no space for God to pour himself into us.

For most of Christian history, fasting has been the practice of abstaining from food.[1] In recent years, however, the definition of fasting has expanded to include abstaining from any number of things—shopping, media, novels, driving, the news, to name a few. Since the purpose of a Lenten fast is to create space in our lives for God, it makes sense that, in our consumption-driven and media-saturated culture, we would fast from things other than food.[2] For we need the space and time to be able to listen to God, as our lives are often too full for us to hear what he might be trying to say. Perhaps the most fruitful of my Lenten fasts was the year I fasted from television. At the time I was watching an hour or two of TV every day. By giving that time to God, I suddenly had a lot more time to study Scripture, pray and play. And that is the aim of the Lenten fast: to create space in our lives for God to have room to enter in.

Once we have that space, we can cultivate it through another traditional Lenten discipline: the prayerful reading and study of Scripture. Since Scripture is one of the primary ways in which God speaks to and educates us, prayerful reading and study give us a chance to listen to what God may be trying to say to us. There is a lovely symbiosis here: by filling the time or space that our fasting has created with Scripture, we open ourselves to having our hunger and thirst for the Word of God reawakened.

By allowing ourselves to be hungry (whether literally hungry for food or figuratively hungry for an experience), we create a space in which another hunger—for God's Word—can arise, and be satisfied.

REPENTANCE

As we have seen, fasting during Lent gives us the opportunity to be intentional about creating space in our lives for God. What we may hear when we stop to listen is that God is calling us to repent of our sin. The cross of ashes on our foreheads that marks the beginning of Lent is no accident. In the Old Testament, people mourned their sin and repented of it in "sackcloth and ashes." So the ashes remind us of the call to repent of our sin, the cause of Christ's death. The liturgical color of the season—purple, the color of repentance—is a reminder of this focus. And, in some traditions, the celebrant says, "Repent and believe the gospel!" (see Mark 1:15) when she imposes the ashes.

For Christians, sin encompasses all in our lives that separates us from Christ. Often these sins are so habitual, so deeply ingrained in our personalities, that they have become part of who we are and we therefore no longer see them for the sin they are. I, for instance, am prone to envy, despair and self-pity. These are not sins that get a lot of press time in our churches or our culture, but they consistently pull my focus off Christ and onto myself, and so I need repeatedly to repent of these habits of thought and heart.

Unfortunately, repentance often leaves a bad taste in people's mouths, as if it conjures up images of self-flagellation, both literal and figurative. I used to think of repentance this way too. As an adolescent, I thought repentance meant reciting unhealthy mantras to convince myself of my own unworthiness (as if I needed to be convinced). As a young adult, I rejected this view of repentance. Actually I rejected repentance altogether, thinking it damaging to my fragile sense of self-worth. And then, the summer I turned thirty, I had my first experience of true repentance.

Every day for an entire month, as I journaled, prayed and read the lectionary, God peeled away layers of myself that I needed to repent of. For the first time in my adult life, I saw the envy, despair and self-pity to which I am prone not as personality quirks but as the sins they are. I knew, more deeply than I had ever known before, that I had failed—failed to love my friends, my husband, my son, myself; failed to pray when I had said I would; failed to even notice the good gift that was my life. Instead, I had complained and whined and been ungrateful and ungracious. I felt deeply convicted of my carelessness, my self-absorption, my *sin*. But I did not feel despair. In fact, I felt freedom—and joy. I cried a lot, to be sure, but they were tears of sorrow *and* gratitude. I felt so grateful that God was showing me all this wretchedness so I could repent of it. I did not want it to be any part of me, and God was graciously taking it away. I had never understood what St. Benedict meant when he called repentance "praying with tears," or even what John the Baptist meant when he called people to repent. Now I did.

There is nothing self-flagellating about repentance. In fact, true repentance is just the opposite: it frees us. When we repent, we acknowledge that we are in bondage to sin, and God, in his mercy and grace, frees us to live as the people we were meant to be. Like fasting, repentance creates space in our lives; it allows us to hear the voice of God speaking to our hearts. Through repentance we become reacquainted with our truest selves, the selves God created in his own image.

CHARITY

In recognizing our sin and, with it, God's mercy, we become able to face—and embrace—the reality that we are utterly dependent on God. The ashen cross we receive on Ash Wednesday, which reminds us of both our origin and our destiny, could be interpreted as a clarion call for charity. For charity begins with humility, the recognition that we share a common origin and a common destiny: we are *all* dust and to dust we shall all return.

The despairing response to this declaration is "Eat, drink, and be merry, for tomorrow we die." The Christian response is to turn, marked as we are with the sign of our mortality, to the Lord's table, where we do indeed eat and drink, but soberly, recognizing in the bread and wine the body and blood of Christ who died that we may live. This is why, on Ash Wednesday, we receive Communion after we are marked with the ashes. As Christians, the declaration of our mortality is not to make us morbid and despairing. It is to remind us who we are—human beings who depend utterly on the mercy and loving-kindness of God. Knowing this, we can extend to others the mercy God has extended to us. We can share our abundance with those in need so that they will have enough (see 2 Corinthians 8:13-14).

One of the practices that has traditionally accompanied the Lenten fast is to take the money saved by not buying food (or books or renting movies or whatever) and give it to a charitable organization, or to a person or family who is in need. This is almsgiving. The purpose of almsgiving, or charity, is the raising up of the lowly and the bringing down of the lofty—not for the sake of role reversal but in order to achieve a fair balance.[3]

One of my favorite stories of this comes from my bibliophilistic friends Ed and Ellie. Ed is a pastor with an interest in naval history.

In addition to all his various commentaries and books on the Christian life, he has a rather extensive collection of books on naval history, some of them quite rare. Ellie is in a Ph.D. program in comparative literature. Her collection of books is also extensive. They estimate they spend, on average, about one hundred dollars a week on books between the two of them.

For Lent several years ago, they decided to fast from buying books and to take the money they would have spent—$650— and give it to a local literacy program. They found this fast so rewarding that they have done it every year since. Last year, they went one step further and volunteered an hour a week at one of the program's reading centers.

THE TRIDUUM

In our corporate worship during Lent, the Lenten cross helps us mark the time as we journey toward Easter. Often made of the trunk of a Christmas tree, the cross has seven purple candles in it, one for each of the Sundays of Lent and one for Maundy Thursday. Whereas in Advent we light one candle each week as we prepare for Christ's coming, in Lent we extinguish one candle each week as we enter ever more deeply into the darkness that will culminate in Christ's death.

I find it interesting that this season of darkness occurs as the days are becoming lighter and longer. Indeed, the word *Lent* itself comes from the Anglo-Saxon word for "lengthen," as in the lengthening of days. The world is celebrating the coming of spring, gushing about the miracle of new life. We Christians aren't there yet. Instead, we seem to be in an ever-darkening, ever-narrowing tunnel, which can end in only one way: our Savior's death on a cross.

At no time in the season is this descent into darkness as obvious as during the Triduum—Maundy Thursday, Good Friday and Holy Saturday—the three days that precede Easter.

Maundy Thursday. Six weeks after Ash Wednesday, I attend another evening service. The church is well lit as the service begins, but slowly, over the course of the readings and songs, the lights dim. When we go forward to receive Communion, only the lights in the choir area at the front of the sanctuary are lit, and, by the end of the service, we are in absolute darkness. Then the church is stripped of its vestments: slowly and silently, the pastor and worship leader cover the chalices and plates of bread, the Bible, the Lenten cross, the processional cross, the altar cloth, even the banners with black cloth. Members of the choir carry each item down the center aisle and out of the sanctuary. Finally, four men lift the Communion table, also draped in a black cloth, and carry it on their shoulders out of the church. They look like pallbearers carrying a coffin.

The congregants sit in the pews, all of us a little stunned by the starkness of it, the finality. No one speaks. There is nothing to say. Then we too begin to leave, filing silently out of the dark sanctuary into the dark night.

Good Friday. On this day of commemorating our Savior's death, it is customary to meditate on what are called the "Seven Last Words," the last utterances of Jesus as he hung on the cross:

- "Father, forgive them; for they know not what they do." (Luke 23:34)[4]
- "Today shalt thou be with me in paradise." (Luke 23:43)
- "Father, into thy hands I commend my spirit." (Luke 23:46)
- "My God, my God, why hast thou forsaken me?" (Matthew 27:46; Mark 15:34)

- "Woman, behold thy son! . . . Behold thy mother!" (John 19:26-27)
- "I thirst." (John 19:28)
- "It is finished." (John 19:30)

Personally I find it overwhelming, even distracting, to try to meditate on all of these, so I will choose just one to ponder, praying the words as a sort of breath prayer as I go through the activities of my day, as a way to remember the passion and crucifixion of Christ.

Holy Saturday. In the Apostles' Creed, we proclaim our belief that after Jesus "suffered under Pontius Pilate, was crucified, dead, and buried, *he descended into hell*" (emphasis mine). Though the descent into hell is part of this most familiar Christian creed, I've not heard much about it in the church circles in which I've lived my life. Indeed, everything I know about it comes from reading in other Christian traditions, especially the Orthodox, which explore this particular article of the creed. Those traditions often locate the descent into hell on Holy Saturday, the day Jesus' body lay in the earth.

The Easter icon of the Orthodox churches is called "The Descent into Hell" and "shows a vigorous Christ astride the fallen cross whose horizontal beams have cleft apart the earth. Visible in the bowels of earth are the enchained mass of the damned who look upward toward their redeemer. Christ, surrounded by the saints, reaches forward and grasps the arm of a person arising out of the grave."[5] This image of Christ striding victoriously into hell and reaching out in love even to the dead and the damned powerfully proclaims, in the words of Wendy Wright, "There is no place God is not."[6] I would add, there is no *time* God is not. On this day of great mourning, shock and devastation over the death of our Lord, even on this day, Christ is at work, loosing the bonds of the prisoners, setting free the captives, raising the dead to new life.

Holy Saturday, then, is a day of contrasts. We mourn our dead Lord even as we prepare for the celebration of his resurrection. We grieve his broken body lying in the tomb even as we celebrate his triumphant march against the gates of hell. We sorrow at the foot of the empty cross even as we anticipate the true and glorious meaning of its emptiness.

THE TABLE OF THE GOOD SHEPHERD

On Ash Wednesday, I had stood at the front of the sanctuary in stunned sadness as the sign of the cross was marked on my forehead. I felt Doug's hand on the small of my back as he gently guided me to the side aisle, where two of our friends were standing. One of them held a plate of bread; the other, a chalice.

As she handed me a piece of bread, my friend spoke to me those oft-repeated words: "The body of Christ, broken for you."

I dipped the bread in the chalice.

"The blood of Christ, poured out for your sake."

And I, the mortal one, received that broken body, that shed blood, which had gained for me immortality.

Death will one day take us all, it is true. But we need not fear it. Though it come, God came first and in Christ has walked through it before us and walks through it with us. The good Shepherd who daily bears our burdens bears this burden as well: he carries us through death and into life.

LIVING THE SEASON

....

The liturgical colors of Lent:
purple (repentance)
black, for the Triduum (death, mourning)

The forty days of Lent find their biblical precedent in the forty days of the flood (Genesis 6–8), the forty days that Moses was on Mount Sinai (Exodus 24:12-18), the forty years of the Israelites' desert wanderings (Numbers 13–33), the forty days of Elijah's journey to Mount Horeb (1 Kings 19:1-12), and Jesus' forty days in the wilderness (Matthew 4:1-11; Mark 1:9-12; Luke 4:1-13). How do the disciplines of fasting, repentance and charity figure into these stories?

Make a Lenten cross. At its simplest, this could be seven purple votives or tea lights arranged in the shape of the cross. If you want to do something more elaborate, make a cross out of two tree branches thick enough in which to drill holes for taper candles. It is traditional to use the trunk or a large branch of your Christmas tree to make this cross, but that is certainly not required. Drill seven holes in the cross—one in each arm and five down the trunk. Place seven purple taper candles in the holes. Light all seven candles each evening (or once a week, if that makes more sense in your life circumstances), then extinguish one candle for each week of Lent that has passed. Extinguish the last candle (usually the center one) on Maundy Thursday. As you watch the light dwindle each week, recall the journey of Christ toward the darkness of Gethsemane and Golgotha. During the Triduum (Maundy Thursday, Good Friday and Holy Saturday), do not light any of the candles. Let the blackened and unlit wicks remind you that the Light has gone out of the world.

Read Matthew 6:1-6, 16-21 (Gospel reading for Ash Wednesday, all years). "Whenever you give alms . . . whenever you pray . . . whenever you fast"—Jesus assumes these are things his followers are doing. As Lent begins, which of these disciplines do you feel Jesus calling you to embrace? In what way will you live out that calling this Lent?

Consider a partial food fast. Traditional items to fast from during Lent include meat, fish, eggs, dairy, sugar and oil. Break your fast (gently; don't binge) on Sundays. The point is not to punish yourself but to create space for God to speak to your spiritual hunger.

Read Psalm 51:1-17 (psalm for Ash Wednesday, all years). What words of this well-known psalm do you most resonate with as you enter and live this season of introspection and repentance? What is God calling you to repent of?

This year on Palm Sunday, I took home one of the palm branches from the children's palm processional at church and stuck it through the knocker on my front door. I wanted to mark Holy Week in a special way and to remember each time I came home that, despite the colored eggs and bunnies that populated every store window I passed, Easter had not yet come.

Read Psalm 116 (psalm for Maundy Thursday, all years.) On this dark day, why this psalm of thanksgiving for deliverance? How could you enter the spirit of the Triduum, with all its attendant darkness, while still keeping your eyes firmly fixed on the end of the story at Easter?

Embrace a no-fire fast during the Triduum: it is traditional not to light a fire on these three days, as a way of remembering that the Light has gone out of the world. One year, I considered turning off the power in my house for these three days, electricity being the modern equivalent of fire, but my husband vetoed that idea. (He is not as into self-deprivation as I am.) So I decided instead that we would not use the stove or oven. I made several salads, some bread and muffins ahead of time.

It was such a small sacrifice—it wasn't even much of a fast, for we ate our fill of salad, cheese and bread at each meal; the only thing I really missed was my morning cup of tea. But it was also profound. For one thing, I had a lot more time in my days because I wasn't cooking. I used that time to really be present with my son, to pray, to read Scripture or poetry. Plus I got to taste, in a very small way, the suffering of Jesus for my sake.

It is of course utterly ludicrous to compare my sacrificing a cup of tea for two days (though I love tea more than the English) with Jesus' death on the cross. And yet, that is part of the gift of fasting. In his grace, God expands our little sacrifices, our small offerings—think of the loaves and fishes—so that they can encompass far more than is possible. My giving up a cup of tea became a tiny icon through which I glimpsed the hugeness of God's love for me.

6 ∘ *Easter*

A Season of Joy

My first year of college was almost unrelentingly miserable. I was painfully shy and felt myself to be invisible. I spent a lot of time hiding in my dorm room, which did nothing to alleviate my loneliness; it only spared me the pain of drifting ghostlike about campus without being seen or acknowledged. Of course, it probably didn't help that, when I did leave my room, I rarely looked at people as they passed me; a preemptive strike, I suppose, against the possibility of their not saying hello, and, like most preemptive strikes, self-defeating and self-fulfilling.

Then, early in winter quarter, I made a friend. She loved books as much as I did, and many of the same ones at that. We read Edgar Allen Poe by candlelight on dark rainy nights and scared ourselves silly. We recalled our girlhood love of *Anne of Green Gables* and laughed over her antics—and our own as we tried to emulate her. We watched *Lady Jane* and cried and cried. We shared our writing with each other, a vulnerable act for us both. We made plans to live together the following year, creating decorating schemes for our dorm room. I went home for spring break walking on air.

When I returned to school, though, something had changed. My friend was not as excited to see me as I was to see her. She began to make excuses for not eating at the same table in the cafeteria. Three weeks into the quarter, she told me she'd decided she didn't want to live in the dorms the following year and was going to rent an apartment with some girls she worked with.

One evening not long after that conversation, I was sitting on my bed reading *The Brothers Karamazov* when someone slipped something under my door. I looked up to see a pink envelope lying on the floor. A sense of foreboding washed over me as I stared at it for a long moment before setting down my book. I walked over, picked it up and opened it. "Dear Kimberlee," it read, "I'm sorry, but I can't be your friend anymore. I've tried these last weeks, but I can no longer pretend that I even like you. You are hurtful and unkind . . ." I read it uncomprehending, and then read it again, as comprehension dawned. And then I cried. I couldn't think what I'd done that was so hurtful or unkind that would make her dislike me so much. And I felt too hurt and betrayed to ask her.

I finished the quarter in a hazy fog of confusion and pain before returning home for the summer, where my parents and sister loved on me and helped me laugh again. Come fall, I did not want to return to school. My father insisted. "If you don't want to go back after Christmas," he promised, "you won't have to. But I want you to give it one more try."

Okay, I thought, *it's only ten weeks. I can do anything for ten weeks.* Still, I cried as I boarded the airplane, and my sense of having been kicked in the stomach only got worse the closer I got to Seattle.

But God, in mercy and grace, had gone before me. On my floor was a girl I'd had several classes with my freshman year, so I immediately recognized her—and to my surprise, she recognized me. Christa and her roommate, Kate, were immensely intelligent and quite witty, which was intimidating—I thought I was nowhere near clever enough to be their friend—but they made it clear they liked me anyway and that, regardless of how I perceived myself, they thought I was plenty smart.

Through Kate and Christa, I made other friends and began to feel part of a community. They invited me to join them when they went to dinner in the cafeteria and included me in outings—to the movies, to readings, to the school play—and in their Shakespeare nights, in which nearly a dozen people crowded into their dorm room to read a play aloud. And every Sunday night, a group of us gathered in their room to watch *Lois and Clark* and eat ice cream.

In looking back, I am amazed by God's goodness to me. I returned to school that fall expecting to experience again the painful loneliness of my freshman year, but instead, I experienced an Easter season of life: God gave me friendship and acceptance where I was expecting isolation and rejection. You might even say God gave me life where I expected death.

The resurrection of Christ is, of course, totally different from anything we can experience in everyday life. Even so, we do get glimpses of the resurrection in the midst of our lives when God surprises us with joy.

THE ORIGINS OF EASTER

Easter—the celebration of Christ's resurrection—is the raison d'être of Christianity. It is the reason Christians worship on Sundays—"the Lord's Day," our early forebears called it. They would gather to reenact the Lord's Supper and recall the amazing triumph of the risen Christ. So this celebration of Christ's resurrection is as old as the church itself, though its formalization as a Christian holy day took many decades.

Early Christians called Easter "Pesach," from the Hebrew name for Passover. In many countries, the name for Easter recalls this connection with Passover—*Pâques* in France, *Påske* in Denmark and *Pascha* in Greece, for example. In English, we lost this linguistic connection when early missionaries to northern Europe and the British Isles renamed this holy day to associate it with the goddess of spring, Eostre, and so make it more appealing to the natives they wanted to convert.

Until 325, Easter was celebrated in conjunction with Passover. At the Council of Nicea, the gathered church leaders agreed that Easter should always be observed on a Sunday and on the same day throughout the church. As a result of the council, Easter came to be (and still is) celebrated on the first Sunday after the first full moon on or after the vernal equinox. Due to this rule, Easter (in the Western church) can fall anytime between March 22 and April 25. Sometimes this coincides with Passover. Often it does not.[1]

From early in Christian tradition, Easter Sunday was the day new converts were baptized, often in catacombs, as a physical reminder that they had died to their old selves and been raised to new life in Christ. During the fourth and fifth centuries, the week after Easter, called the Easter octave, was a time of intensive instruction for these newly baptized, who continued to wear their white baptismal robes for the entire week as a symbol of their new life.

By the mid-fourth century, the Great Fifty Days (so called because the Easter season stretches from Easter Sunday to

Pentecost seven weeks, or fifty days, later) were already observed as a time of sustained attention to the reality and joy of resurrection. Each of the Sundays of Easter echoes the great celebration of Easter Sunday itself. The return of the word *alleluia* to worship services after its absence through the weeks of Lent serves as a reminder of Easter joy, as does the call and response of the Easter refrain, joyfully proclaimed on each of the season's Sundays:

Christ is risen!
He is risen indeed!
Christ is risen!
He is risen indeed!
Christ is risen!
Alleluia! He is risen indeed!

Easter's liturgical color is white, often embellished with gold, and the white banners, altar cloths and vestments remain in the sanctuary throughout the season. White is the color of purity and joy; gold, of royalty and triumph. Together these colors remind us that the risen Christ reigns in majesty, interceding on our behalf, forgiving our sins and transforming us into his likeness that we might be pure, like unalloyed gold—and that is cause for the greatest joy.

EASTER DAY—AND BEYOND

In the Greek Orthodox Church, congregants gather outside the church building before daybreak on Easter morning. Holding lit candles, they wait in the darkness. Then someone in the crowd knocks on the door of the church and calls out, "Is Jesus inside?" From within comes the response: "No, he is not here. He is risen!" The door is flung open and the people enter with joy, their candles illuminating the dark sanctuary.

In other traditions, congregants gather for the Easter Vigil, sometimes just after nightfall on Holy Saturday and sometimes in the wee hours of Easter morning, to wait through the darkness for the dawn of Easter. Wendy Wright describes such a service in her book *The Rising*:

> We begin the vigil in the depths of night as we have since the beginnings of the church. The sanctuary is swallowed in darkness. All wait in the pregnant silence. Then the paschal candle is lit and the celebrant proclaims, "Christ our light." From that one candle is ignited each of the small candles those in the congregation hold. The shadowy church is gradually illuminated by the light from hundreds of flickering tapers. The radiance of the dawning resurrection light transfigures the night.[2]

I confess I have never experienced Easter in this way. By the time I learned that Christians did such beautiful things, I had a baby whose crying and fussing would have distracted me (and everyone around me) from being fully present to the meaning of the liturgy.

Then my friend Matt, who was raised in a church he says was suffocating in its own liturgy, told me about his decision to have a different sort of Easter vigil: he took his dog for a walk around the neighborhood after nightfall on Holy Saturday. The next morning, he woke up early, before the sun rose, and took her for another walk. "It was so cool," he recounted, "to go out on Saturday and be in the darkest part of Lent, and then to wake up the next morning and be in Easter." He and his dog walked in the brisk morning air, watching the world grow lighter and brighter until the sun appeared over the horizon. He experienced in a small but meaningful way the return of light after the darkness of Lent and, particularly, the Triduum.

When I heard this story, I promised myself that next year (since my children will still be too little to go to an Easter Vigil) I will go for a predawn walk. I will watch the sun rise. I will contemplate the amazing reality of resurrection. I will feel the incredible joy and wonder of Easter.

The Gospels, especially Mark, record the astonishment of the original hearers of the good news that Jesus was raised from the dead. Alas, in the church we have heard the story so often that the amazement of the women at the tomb, of the disciples in the upper room, of Cleopas and his companion on the road to Emmaus is a little confusing to us. The Easter message of resurrection has become so familiar it has lost its power to amaze and inspire us, which is a large part of the reason I long for the experience of waiting and watching through the darkness of Holy Saturday night for the light of Easter morning. I think such an experience will jolt me out of my passive, thoughtless acceptance, my habitual nod of affirmation in the direction of Easter.

The closest I've come to the astonishment of the disciples when they heard the good news of Jesus' resurrection occurred the Easter my son was two. Jack's Sunday school teacher had brought a huge bouquet of helium balloons and let each child choose one to take home. Jack chose red. Proudly and joyfully, he carried his bobbing balloon down the church hallway to the Fellowship Hall, where Doug and I stopped to chat with our associate pastor, Steve, and his wife about our recent visit to Steve's hometown. A few minutes into our conversation, Jack let out a piercing wail. He had let go of his balloon, and it had floated to the top of the Fellowship Hall, some twelve feet above our heads.

"Oh sweetie." I picked Jack up as he began to sob. "That's so sad."

Steve said to Jack, "Hey, pal, don't worry. I'll go get a ladder. We'll get it down."

"No, please," I said. "Please don't. We believe in letting him experience the consequences of his actions."

But Steve had already headed across the Fellowship Hall in search of a ladder. He turned around. "It's Easter, Kimberlee. There are no consequences."

I stared after him, my mouth half-open to voice an objection that died on my lips. Steve got Jack's balloon down, and I hope and pray that deep in his being, my son now knows something it will take me the rest of my life to believe: the resurrection changes everything. Everything. The reality of Easter—Christ risen, death defeated, sins forgiven, evil overcome, no consequences—is so incredible, in the original sense of the word, that it's beyond believable.

This is why I need more than just Easter Day. If Easter were only a single day, I would never have time to let its incredible reality settle over me, settle into me. I would trudge through my life with a disconnect between what I say I believe about resurrection and how I live (or fail to live) my life in light of it. Thanks be to God, our forebears in faith had people like me in mind when they decided we simply cannot celebrate Easter in a single day, or even a single week. No, they decided, we need fifty days, seven Sundays, to even begin to plumb the depths of this event. They knew, as we too often do not, that the riches of this most important event in all of history cannot be exhausted in a single day.

In contemporary America, Protestant Christians, like drug-store card racks, all too often move on to Mother's Day as soon as Easter Day has passed. But we do so at our peril. We risk relegating

the most important event in all history to a single day, something
we celebrate with a church full of lilies, some great music and
a sermon about that first Easter before we clear out the lilies
after the services, disband the Easter choir and, for all practical
purposes, forget about resurrection for another year.

We need the season of Easter, the Great Fifty Days, to live with
the mystery of resurrection for a while, to let the magnitude of it
dawn on us, dawn *in* us.

THE ROAD TO EMMAUS

The purpose of the season of Easter, it seems to me, is to give
us the time we need to absorb the reality that Christ is risen.
Wendy Wright says, "The very idea of resurrection shatters all the
categories of comprehension with which we make sense of our
world. It draws us instead into a reality that transcends present
possibility. . . . [At the empty tomb] we are met, at the far limits of
our resources, with limitlessness."[3] Such a radical re-visioning of
the world—a world without consequences—requires time. We
need time so that our eyes might learn to see the risen Christ,
our hearts to believe that he is risen indeed. We need time to
be encountered by the risen Christ, and we need time for that
encounter to transform us from people who say we believe to
people who enflesh and embody that belief.

The two followers of Jesus who leave Jerusalem for Emmaus
that first Sunday after Jesus' crucifixion need time too.[4] Their
faces as they walk, Luke tells us, are downcast because they had
hoped Jesus was the Messiah who was going to redeem Israel. They
had hoped. But no longer. Jesus is dead, crucified like a common
criminal. Their hopes for redemption are dashed, shattered, by
that cruel reality.

When the risen Jesus encounters them, they do not recognize him. Now, these two had heard the women's report: how Mary and the others had gone to the grave, but Jesus' body was not there; instead, they saw angels who told them he was alive. They had also heard Peter's testimony, how he too had seen the empty tomb and the scattered strips of linen in which Jesus' dead body had been wrapped.

In spite of these reports, these two are still despairing, their hopes still shattered, their eyes unable to recognize Jesus. Did they not believe the women and Peter? Maybe they wanted to believe, but were afraid to. Or maybe they did believe but did not grasp the magnitude of what the women were proclaiming. Regardless, it is their *encounter* with the risen Christ that transforms their despair into joy, that transforms them from people who doubt to people who believe and joyfully proclaim the good news.[5]

Every year when Easter Sunday comes around, I find that I too am on the road to Emmaus. I am not yet ready to see the risen Christ. I am still in a Lenten mode—introspective, penitent, self-denying—and it is hard for me to grasp the reality of Easter, which always seems to take me by surprise. It is not that I don't believe the message of this season—Christ is risen! He is risen indeed! I do believe it, at least on some level. I am willing to affirm it, to speak it, even to proclaim it. But mostly I don't *live* like it's true.

Like the disciples trudging up the road to Emmaus, I trudge through life as if Easter were just a nice day in spring and not the earth-shaking, mind-blowing, life-altering, cosmos-shattering event that it is. Like these disciples, I am encountered by the risen Christ and am so self-absorbed I do not recognize him. Like them, I pour out my complaints, my heartbreak, my disappointed hopes. And as he did with them, Jesus patiently bears with my foolishness, my slowness of heart. Again and again, year after year, he uses these days and weeks of Easter to walk me through the Scriptures that I might learn to see anew that indeed he is risen, and he uses the breaking of the bread in the Lord's Supper to make himself known to me.

I began to understand experientially the wisdom of the Great Fifty Days the year after my son was born. As the darkness of my postpartum depression gradually lifted during the days and weeks of Easter that year, I wrote in a note to friends who had walked with me and prayed for me in that difficult time: "I feel I have finally emerged into the light again, my own personal Eastertide."

To be sure, there was nothing gradual about Christ's resurrection. But for me as Jesus' follower, the realization of resurrection is a gradual one, a dawning understanding I must live into as I proclaim week after week, "Christ is risen! Alleluia! He is risen indeed!"—until this amazing proclamation settles into my soul and permeates every fiber of my being.

DANCING

It's Easter, Kimberlee. There are no consequences. I am still pondering Steve's words to me that Easter morning. I expect I will ponder them for a long time to come. What does it mean to live in the reality of Easter, a reality in which there are no consequences? I confess I don't know. My suspicion, though, is that it looks a lot different from the way I usually live my life: a lot freer, bolder, more gracious and generous, and a lot less afraid.

To live in the reality of Easter is to affirm with our lives that whatever evil things befall us, God has already beaten them. In Jesus, all our rejection, loneliness and self-recrimination, everything that's haunting us, scaring us or causing us pain has already been trampled underfoot. These things are already defeated. "Jesus," says Wendy Wright, "was the one who danced on his own grave. With nimble feet, he rose up prancing, trampling death and sorrow underfoot. At Easter we are invited to do the same. All in our lives that is limiting, sorrowful, or dead becomes the dance floor on which we celebrate our Easter joy."[6]

It is Christ's triumph over death and evil that makes it possible for us to live the rest of the church year, which is a metaphor for the whole of our lives: the time between Christ's dance on *his* grave at Easter and his dance on *all* our graves when he comes again as Christ the King.

LIVING THE SEASON

....

The liturgical colors of Easter:
white (purity, joy)
gold (royalty, triumph)

Read Mark 16:1-8 (Gospel reading for Easter Day, year B). Mark ended his Gospel here, with the terrified women fleeing from the empty tomb. Why were they so afraid? Why does Mark leave us with this image of Jesus' amazed disciples saying nothing about what they have seen? In the church we have heard the resurrection story so often that we are no longed amazed by it. What will you do in the weeks of Easter to recapture a sense of the women's amazement?

Instead of greeting family, friends and people at church on Easter Sunday with a bland "Happy Easter," greet them with "Christ is risen!" When I called my mother this year on Easter, these were the first words I said when she answered the phone. I could hear the smile in her voice as she responded, "He is risen indeed!"

Read Jeremiah 31:1-6 (Old Testament reading for Easter Day, year A). Where in your life has God surprised you with "grace in the wilderness"? How can these experiences help you enter into the amazing, surprising joy that characterizes the Easter season?

My friend Ellie refrains from having flowers in her home during the weeks of Lent. Then, on Easter Day and throughout the season, she goes crazy with the flowers, filling vases on her dining table, sideboard, mantle, kitchen counter and desk. The flowers remind her that, in and through the resurrection, Christ has given us new life and given it abundantly.

Read Psalm 23 (psalm for fourth Sunday of Easter, all years) and John 10:11-18
(Gospel reading for fourth Sunday of Easter, year B). The image of Christ as the
good Shepherd is a familiar one. How does placing this image at the center of the
Easter season shape, expand or deepen your understanding of resurrection joy?

At your household meal each day (or week) during Easter, light a
white candle and say the Easter greeting together.

> Leader: Christ is risen!
> Others: Alleluia! He is risen indeed!

Or you could use this prayer: "Christ has become our paschal
sacrifice; let us feast with joy in the Lord. Alleluia!"[7]

Read 1 John (over the Sundays of Easter, we read through the whole of this epistle,
all years). How does reading this "epistle of love" during Easter change the way you
read it? How does it change the way you receive or think about Easter?

7 ∘ *Pentecost*

Power and Beauty

My dear friend Susan was coming home to Seattle from Boston, where she is in a Ph.D. program. A nervous flyer, she had historically taken the bus or the train when she traveled. This time, though, she was eager to be home and decided she couldn't spend five of her precious vacation days on the train, so she bought a plane ticket. The evening I was supposed to pick her up, I was getting ready to cut out of a meeting early when she called me. "Are you here already?" I asked when I answered my phone.

She laughed, nervously. "Um, no. I'm in Texas."

"Texas?" Her parents live in Texas. Had she changed her itinerary and forgotten to tell me?

"There are thunderstorms all through the Midwest. We had to fly further and further south to try to go around them, but they kept coming south too. We had to stop here to refuel." Susan's fear of flying had originated from taking off in a thunderstorm and all the turbulence that ensued as the pilot fought to keep the plane on course in the heavy wind and rain.

"Are you okay?" I asked, imagining she was near tears.

A moment of silence. "Yeah, actually, I am."

"Are you really? Or are you putting on a brave face?"

Susan laughed. "Probably a little of each. I'll tell you all about it when I get there." She gave me her new arrival information.

At midnight, I drove to the airport to pick her up. She was exhausted, but exhilarated. "The thunderstorms were beautiful!" She'd had a window seat and could watch the storm clouds forming in the distance. "Their tops were perfectly flat, and they were dark but with this amazing red glow. When the lightning flashed, they would become brilliant with light. It was stunning."

"It sounds scary." I'm a nervous flyer too.

"Yes," Susan said, thoughtfully. "It was. But it was so beautiful, I forgot to be afraid most of the time."

Stunning and scary. Beautiful and powerful. Wild and luminous. These words strike me as reflecting the paradox of the Holy Spirit, whose outpouring on the followers of Jesus we celebrate on Pentecost.

THE ORIGINS OF PENTECOST

According to the Gospels, Jesus appeared to his disciples for forty days before he ascended to the Father. In the church, Ascension is celebrated on the seventh and final Sunday of Easter. (Technically Ascension is the Thursday before, but because many churches do not have daily services, it is usually celebrated on Sunday.) After Jesus' ascension, his followers returned to Jerusalem to await the Counselor he had promised to send. On Pentecost, Acts tells us, they were gathered together.

Pentecost is the Greek name for a Jewish holy day. According to Leviticus 23, on the Sunday after Passover (the day of Christ's resurrection), the grain harvest was to begin and a sheaf of barley, the first grain to be harvested, was to be taken to the temple as the firstfruits offering to the Lord. Seven sabbaths (or fifty days) later, at the commencement of the wheat harvest, a second grain offering was to be brought to the temple. This feast of the harvest was called *Shavuoth,* that is, "weeks," in Hebrew. The Greek word *Pentecost* means "fiftieth." On this day, Jews celebrate not just the harvest but also the giving of the Torah to Moses on Mount Sinai. Thus, Jesus' followers were gathered on Pentecost to commemorate the gift of the Law, when

> suddenly from heaven there came a sound like the rush of a violent wind, and it filled the entire house where they were sitting. Divided tongues, as of fire, appeared among them, and a tongue rested on each of them. All of them were filled with the Holy Spirit and began to speak in other languages, as the Spirit gave them ability. (Acts 2:2-4)

The celebration of Pentecost as a Christian holy day began in New Testament times. Given the largely Jewish makeup of the early church, Pentecost was originally associated with Shavuoth, and the outpouring of the Holy Spirit made that holy day even more important and meaningful. Just as the giving of the Torah to Moses constituted the birth of Israel as a nation and inaugurated their identity as Yahweh's covenant people, so the giving of the Holy Spirit to the disciples constituted the birth of the church and inaugurated their identity as the body of Christ. Over the next few centuries, as the church became more separated from its Jewish origins, Pentecost lost its character as a commemoration of the giving of the Torah and became exclusively about the outpouring of the Holy Spirit.

From as early as the third century, Pentecost was one of
the chief holy days of the church, with some church fathers
proclaiming it the highest of church feasts. Over time, Pentecost,
like other high holy days, came to be celebrated not just for a
day but for eight days, from Sunday to Sunday. The Sunday after
Pentecost, called Trinity Sunday or Whitsunday (White Sunday,
because of the white altar cloths and banners), is thus both the
beginning of Ordinary Time and, with its focus on the Trinity,
an appropriate conclusion to the octave (eight days) of Pentecost,
during which we celebrate the outpouring and indwelling of
the third Person of the Trinity. The liturgical color of Pentecost
is red, a reminder of the Holy Spirit's descent like "tongues, as
of fire" on the gathered disciples.

THE WILDNESS OF GOD

Many themes emerge from the story of Pentecost, among them
the interrelated mysteries of God's power and of the church as
Christ's body. A pastor friend of mine says that, in her experience,
cradle Christians are uncomfortable with the Holy Spirit—too
messy, uncontrollable, unpredictable, too *wild*—whereas seekers
are drawn to him. Seekers assume that if God is real, then of
course God will be powerful; of course we will see signs and
wonders in his presence. As Lydia, an artist who came to faith in
her twenties, told me, "I love that crazy unexpectedness of the
Holy Spirit."

Unlike Lydia, I admit I am afraid of the powerful image of the
Holy Spirit portrayed in the Pentecost story. The Holy Spirit as
Comforter and Counselor is more my style. The Holy Spirit as
a violent wind breathing tongues of fire on the people of God,
filling them so full they overflow with words in languages they

don't know—this scares me. I want to see the Holy Spirit at work, transforming lives, drawing all people to Christ, changing hearts, comforting the afflicted, convicting the avaricious and the apathetic. Of course I want that. I just want it on my terms— slow and quiet. And a lot of the time, that's how the Holy Spirit seems to work—slowly, inwardly, quietly, subtly, in ways that are not easily discerned unless one is paying attention or taking a long view of things.

But sometimes the Holy Spirit is loud, raucous, obvious, even violent, as in the Pentecost story. Sometimes the Spirit comes with signs and wonders, as Peter proclaims when he quotes the prophet Joel: the sun turns "to darkness and the moon to blood" (Acts 2:20). Sometimes the Spirit is a lot more like a thunderstorm than a gentle breeze. There is, to my mind, nothing comforting about such an image. It is terrifying. Powerful. Wild. I picture upheaval and destruction. These are not images of God and God's way of being with us that I like. But they are present throughout Scripture, and so we must reckon with them and allow our vision of God to be big enough to include this wild and even terrifying aspect of God's nature.

C. S. Lewis captures this wildness of the Holy Spirit in the second book of his Chronicles of Narnia. The human heroines, Lucy and Susan, are with Aslan, a great lion and the story's Christ figure, as he reclaims the country of Narnia from the rule of an evil usurper king. In the course of their adventures with Aslan, the two girls encounter

> a youth, dressed only in a fawn-skin with vine leaves wreathed in his curly hair. His face would have been almost too pretty for a boy's, if it had not looked so extremely wild.

You felt, as Edmund [their brother] said when he saw him a few days later, "There's a chap who might do anything— absolutely anything."[1]

With the boy are a number of girls, "as wild as he."[2] They sing and play music and dance wildly, vines laden with ripe fruit trailing in their wake and growing everywhere. The scene is one of wildness and chaos and joyful euphoria. Later, at Aslan's command, the boy and his girls weave their vines along a bridge, to free the river god trapped by its weight:

> [The boy] and his people splashed forward into the shallow water, and a minute later the most curious things began happening. Great, strong trunks of ivy came curling up all the piers of the bridge, growing as quickly as a fire grows, wrapping the stones round, splitting, breaking, separating them. The walls of the bridge turned into hedges gay with hawthorn for a moment and then disappeared as the whole thing with a rush and a rumble collapsed into the swirling water. With much splashing, screaming, and laughter the revelers waded or swam or danced across the ford.[3]

This boy, it turns out, is Bacchus; his girls, the Maenads. Upon this discovery, Susan says to Lucy, "I say, Lu . . . I wouldn't have felt safe with Bacchus and all his wild girls if we'd met them without Aslan." To which Lucy responds, "I should think not."[4]

I'm of Susan's mind. I think the wildness and power of God, seen especially in the Person of the Holy Spirit, would be unbearable were it not for Jesus. In saying this, I am not implying that Jesus was the good-buddy nice-guy he is too often portrayed as these days. No, Jesus too showed incredible power, as when he cleared the temple with a whip of cords. He had harsh words for many people and hard, uncomfortable words for many others. He is very much in line with this God who is wilder than we like to imagine, who is all-powerful and untamable. But in Jesus, God limits his boundless wildness so we can know that he is *good,* so we can see his heart is *for* us. This does not mean encounters with this wild, powerful God are not frightening—they certainly can be. It *does* mean we can trust God in the midst of our fear because God's heart is a heart of love, overflowing for us, overflowing *into* us.

THE BODY OF CHRIST

This overflowing love created the church: on Pentecost, the Holy Spirit swooped in with wild joy and delight, the abundant love of God poured out on mortals. Because of that outpouring, the Holy Spirit dwells with us, in us. We, like Mary, have become God-bearers. We bear God to all whom we encounter. This is a great privilege and a grave responsibility. Too often we forget we are God-bearers and live and speak in ways that misrepresent God to the world.

Thanks be to God, none of us is an exclusive bearer of God. In fact, we bear God better together; as the church, the people of God, we bear God more completely (though always *in*completely, never fully) because God, too, is community. On the Sunday after Pentecost, Trinity Sunday, we celebrate Christianity's unique view of God as the Three-in-One. In the mystery of the Trinity, we see that God, in his very being, is relational, is a community. One of my favorite images of the Trinity is of a dance, each Person of the Trinity interpenetrating the Others in the self-giving dance of divine love, so woven together as to be inseparable, as to be One.

Meditating on this reality on the Sunday after Pentecost strikes me as a good way to deepen our appreciation for the church, whose birth we celebrate on Pentecost, for, created in the image of this communal God, we human beings need to know and be known by others in deep and meaningful ways. We need the church, the community of people who seek to know and love this triune God, to walk in God's ways, and to follow God's commands. In this community, despite its faults, flaws and failures, our longing to know and be known can be nourished, tastes of belonging can whet our appetites for life in the coming kingdom of God, and love for God and others can usher us ever deeper into the mystery of the Trinity.

In this community, those who do not know God can glimpse his nature as a community of love and be drawn into that community, for the people of God, through the outpouring of the Holy Spirit, are transformed into the very body of Christ. In the church, we bandy this phrase about so much that we fail to really think about its implications, to be amazed by the reality it points to—we become the *body* of Christ; and since Christ is God, then in some mystical, mysterious way, we, all of us together, become one with God! This is a great mystery, and a cause for great celebration.

SPEAKING IN TONGUES

A friend of mine, whose faith and life I greatly esteem, has frequently told me that all Christians should pray to receive the gift the disciples received on Pentecost—that is, to speak in tongues. After all, the prophet Joel (whom the apostle Peter quotes in his Pentecost sermon) proclaims that God will pour out his Spirit on *all* flesh (see Acts 2:17). And Paul says that the Spirit gives good gifts to *everyone* (see 1 Corinthians 12:7). Speaking in tongues, whether that's a prayer language spoken in the interior of one's heart or a more prophetic word given in the midst of the gathered faithful, is assuredly a powerful manifestation of the Spirit's presence. It would also be a lovely and deeply meaningful way to enter into and live the spirit of Pentecost.

That said, I realize that not every Christian has been graced with this gift. I know this because I am one of them. Believing my friend to be correct in his claim that Christians should pray for this particular manifestation of the Spirit, I have prayed for the gift of tongues, but it has not been given. Perhaps this is because speaking in tongues is a gift, and a gift by its very nature is not given to all but only to those whom God chooses. Or perhaps the reason is that even in those moments when I've most wanted this gift, most fervently prayed for it, I've been afraid to receive it: I'd rather fly around the storm, no matter how beautiful it is, than straight into its heart.

Regardless of the reason I have not received this gift, it has been helpful to remember that the gift of tongues is not the only gift Paul mentions. In his list of gifts, he includes the utterance of wisdom, the utterance of knowledge, faith, gifts of healing, the working of miracles, prophecy, the discernment of spirits and the interpretation of tongues (see 1 Corinthians 12:7-10). It has also been helpful to know faithful, mature and wise lovers of Jesus who, like me, do not speak in tongues. They remind me that all the gifts of the Spirit are good, that God gives them to whom he chooses and that my task is not to bemoan my lack of this one gift but to use the gifts I have been given for "the common good" (1 Corinthians 12:7).

I am convinced God has a sense of humor and delights in impeccable timing, for, in the midst of writing this chapter on Pentecost, I had what I can only describe as an enspirited experience. No, I did not receive the gift of tongues. I was asked to preach at my church. I was so nervous the Sunday I preached that I sat in the front row of pews instead of in the preacher's chair on the dais—I didn't want the whole congregation to see me crying. When I stepped into the pulpit, I was trembling. But then I prayed aloud for the Holy Spirit to come and speak through the words I had prepared. And he did! I cannot articulate what happened. I only know that I was able to get out of the way, that the words I had written seemed to speak themselves through me, that something—Someone—larger and more powerful than I am was at work in the words I was speaking. At the end of the sermon, I felt euphoric, heady with amazement—*enspirited*. For the first time, I experienced why people long for the gift of tongues—it is such a concrete, obvious manifestation of the Spirit, and the Spirit's felt presence creates an incredible sense of rightness and joy.

In spite of my fear, then—in the midst of it even—God works. The Holy Spirit works in ways that don't frighten me, that don't make me flee, transforming me slowly but surely into the likeness of Christ, so that I may more truly bear God's image to the world. Eventually (I hope) I will trust God enough to believe with my whole being that letting the Spirit fill me to overflowing will not wash away my self but will give my true self—the self created in God's image—back to me. Then I will finally know that the heart of the storm is the safest place to be.

LIVING THE SEASON

The liturgical color of Pentecost:
red (fire)

It is customary to wear red to church on Pentecost. Lydia, an artist, had a pair of red high-tops that she wore each year on Pentecost—and only on that day.

Read Acts 2:1-21 (epistle reading for Pentecost, all years). How do you respond to God's outpouring of the Holy Spirit? Do you resonate with Lydia's love of the Spirit's "crazy unexpectedness"? Are you more like me, inclined to view the Spirit's wildness with wariness? What about the Holy Spirit draws you into the love of God? What, if anything, about the Spirit keeps you away?

Throughout the octave of Pentecost (from Pentecost Sunday through the next Sunday), light a red candle at your household meal each day.

Read Ezekiel 37:1-14 (Old Testament reading for Pentecost, year B). What does the Spirit do in this passage? How do the Spirit's actions in this story help you understand the ways in which Pentecost is the culmination of the Easter season?

One symbol frequently associated with the Holy Spirit is the dove. In the Middle Ages, it was customary to hang a carved wooden dove above the dining table. Try this or some variation of it—a picture of a dove, perhaps. You could leave the dove out throughout Ordinary Time as well, as a reminder that, thanks to the gift of the Holy Spirit on Pentecost, God is present in all times and all places.[5]

Read 1 Corinthians 12:3b-13 (epistle reading for Pentecost, year A). How comfortable are you with these gifts of the Spirit? Are there gifts that seem more important than others? Why? What gifts have you been given? What gifts do you long for God to give you? Why? How can you recognize and celebrate all these gifts and the people to whom they have been given during the octave (eight days) of Pentecost?

8 ∘ *Ordinary Time*

Transfiguration

After my son was born, I experienced a deep depression. I cried a lot. Jack cried more and would not be comforted. I felt impotent and enraged and wanted to hit him, which made me afraid to pick him up. Instead, I hid under my covers weeping while he lay in his crib wailing. After what seemed like hours of this, but was probably only minutes, I crept into his room, feeling guilty and contrite, held him tenderly, protectively, and we cried together. I lived with a constant sense of fear, anxiety and sadness that erupted into full-blown panic whenever I thought of the future, of days like this, full of emotional instability and sometimes overwhelming sadness, stretching out endlessly before me.

In the midst of that time, which I mostly remember as if it were shrouded in thick, dark clouds, I can recall one moment when those clouds parted and I was able to see a reality beyond the one in which I was trapped. It happened, of all places, in the kitchen. I was washing a bunch of Swiss chard in the sink when suddenly I became aware of how beautiful it was—the crinkly, dark green leaves with their bright red veins, the thick yet silky texture of the leaf as I gently pulled apart each fold to wash inside it, the way the leaves glistened in the sunlight slanting through the kitchen window as I lifted each washed leaf out of the water and placed it on the towel beside the sink. Time seemed to stop—or at least cease to matter—as I wondered at the beauty of the chard.

I had washed chard countless times before this and have done so scores of times since, and I have not been able to re-create this experience. I can notice the contrast of green and red, the silky texture of the leaves, the water drops clinging to them, but I cannot reproduce the sense of awe and timelessness and holiness I felt that day. Sometimes the world simply unfolds its mystery and we happen to be in the right place at the right time and in the right emotional or spiritual space to notice the mystery, to receive it, to be encountered by it.

GLIMPSES OF GLORY

When I was a girl, I longed to experience what Emily Starr, the heroine of L. M. Montgomery's Emily trilogy, called "the flash":

> It had always seemed to Emily, ever since she could remember, that she was very, very near to a world of wonderful beauty. Between it and herself hung only a thin curtain; she could never draw the curtain aside—but sometimes, just for a moment, a wind fluttered it and then it was as if she caught a glimpse of the enchanting realm beyond—only a glimpse—and heard a note of unearthly music. . . . And always when the flash came to her Emily felt that life was a wonderful, mysterious thing of persistent beauty.[1]

I wanted to experience that glimpse of the transcendent, to be thrilled with the momentary parting of the veil between heaven and earth.

What I have since realized is that I do have these glimpses of the glory beyond and that they are a mixed blessing. The parting of the veil fills me with awe and delights my soul, but it also opens in me a yearning, a deep and almost painful desire. For in glimpsing this fleeting beauty, I become aware of a mystery—that there is more to life than usually meets the eye—and I yearn to enter more deeply into that mystery and to live in those moments that shimmer with a radiance that is beyond what we usually see or know.

In the past, I have grasped at whatever ushered me into the enchanted realm beyond the veil—the sleeve of my husband's crisply striped shirt, the roses fresh-cut from my rosebushes and sitting in a bowl on the counter, the crescendo of the organ as we sing the name of Jesus in church—in an attempt to replicate the experience and so quench my desire to live in moments of mystery. This never works. After the moment has passed, the thing itself is a reminder of what I once saw or felt or heard, but it can no longer usher me into that other realm. Now I mostly know better than to pick roses with the expectation that they will open a window on mystery. I've learned that I can never enter that other realm by contrivance or simply because I want to. I can only try to pay attention, because I never know when or where the veil might part and mystery might unfold before me.

ORDINARY TIME REVISITED: TRANSFIGURATION
The weeks between Pentecost and the first Sunday of Advent comprise the second cycle of Ordinary Time. Smack dab in the middle of this season, on August 6, comes the Feast of the Transfiguration, one of my favorite holy days. In some traditions,

Transfiguration is celebrated the Sunday before Ash Wednesday.
Either way, it falls during Ordinary Time, a profound reminder
that when mystery confronts us, it is often when we least expect
it—God takes the ordinary moments of our lives and transforms
them into something holy.

I imagine that when Jesus takes Peter, James and John up on
Mount Tabor to pray, the disciples are not expecting to glimpse
the mystery of the incarnation.[2] How many times had these
disciples prayed with Jesus in the months or years they followed
him? Dozens? Hundreds? And never before had the appearance of
his face changed and his clothes become dazzling white. Never
before had Moses and Elijah appeared with him in glory. So it
is hardly surprising that Peter, James and John are half-asleep as
Jesus prays through the night. Only when they fully awaken do
they come face to face with mystery: they see Jesus in his glory,
a glory that is his from before time, but which has been veiled
from their sight until this moment when they finally see him as
he truly is.

As Moses and Elijah are about to leave, Peter bursts out in his
impetuous way, "Master, it is good for us to be here; let us make
three dwellings, one for you, one for Moses, and one for Elijah"
(Luke 9:33). He wants this moment to last, I think, but he also,
instinctively, wants to contain their glory. And no wonder—
perhaps he knows that we mortals can bear only so much
reality before it overwhelms our senses. Perhaps this is why the
disciples are terrified as they enter the cloud. They know that
the cloud signals the presence of God,[3] and they know that no
one can look on God and live. It is not simply because we are
sinful and God is holy. No, it is because God is real, and our
finite minds cannot comprehend nor our frail bodies bear the

eternity and majesty—the utter realness—of God.

I began to understand this fear of God experientially nearly a decade ago when I took a trip to the Olympic Peninsula from my home in Seattle. As I drove up to Hurricane Ridge, I stopped along the side of the road and got out of my car to look at the mountains. I gazed at the enormous peaks and valleys that rose and fell before me in breathtaking beauty all the way to the horizon, and I began to shiver in spite of the warm August sun. I was, in truth, terrified. In the face of such vastness, such ancient and incomprehensible substantiality, I felt my own smallness and insignificance. I tried to make myself stand there and reckon with the terror I felt in the presence of a world far older and more tremendous than the one I had known only moments before, but I could not. I turned my back on the mountains and fled to the seeming safety of my car.

In our finitude and weakness, we cannot bear to look on ultimate reality any more than we can bear to look directly at the sun. And so reality is veiled, hidden from view—at least most of the time. But every so often, we, like Emily and the disciples, glimpse the enchanted realm beyond the veil. We see, for a fleeting moment, the glory of God made manifest among us. We encounter mystery—or rather, it encounters us.

THE QUOTIDIAN MYSTERIES

While we cannot force an encounter with mystery, we can be open to receiving one. We can learn to pay attention, especially in the midst of those daily tasks we do so often that they become rote and mindless. Kathleen Norris, in her book *The Quotidian Mysteries,* suggests:

> it is in the routine and the everyday that we find the
> possibilities for the greatest transformation. . . . What we
> think we are only "getting through" has the power to
> change us. . . . What we dread as mindless activity can free
> us, mind and heart, for the workings of the Holy Spirit.[4]

It is in the quotidian that mystery most often unfolds, as it did
for me that day at the kitchen sink, as it did for the disciples who
were trying to pray.

We live the bulk of our lives in the daily, doing the same tasks
again and again—preparing food, showering, dressing, checking
voicemail or email, doing dishes or laundry, commuting to
work—and it can come to feel like a grind, pointless and
redundant. But it is precisely because these tasks are daily that
they have such transformative potential. Such work has "an
intense relation with the present moment, a kind of faith in the
present that fosters hope and makes life seem possible in the
day-to-day."[5] And it is only in the present moment that the veil
can part. It is in the daily, ordinary moments of our lives where
we have the most opportunity to notice mystery, to encounter
it and to be encountered by it.

Now, sometimes mystery forces itself on us, even if we're
not paying attention, shaking us by the shoulders as it were
and crying, "Look! Listen!" I've found, though, that the more
closely I attend to the world around me—noticing the curve of
my son's smile, the particular pitch of my daughter's voice, the
even rhythm of the cat's breathing as he lies beside me on the
sofa, the slant of sunshine on the dining room wall, the bright
purple berries on a bush outside my window, the joyful bark of
my husband's laugh—the more likely I am to receive a glimpse

of the glory beyond this world. For in sharpening our physical senses to be more aware of this world, we are also quickening our spirits, opening them to the earthly beauty that surrounds us so that we will be more ready to receive visions of the unearthly beauty that lies just beyond our senses on the other side of the veil. As with any grace, we cannot force or demand such a vision. We can only wait for it, attentively and hopefully, as we engage in the relationships and work that constitute our lives.

In this waiting, we see through a glass, darkly. But occasionally the glass clears, the veil parts, and we see more fully, more truly, more real-ly than we usually do. These glimpses through the glass, beyond the veil, are what sustain us, filling us with hope that, ultimately, all will be well. When I encountered mystery in the shape and hue of chard leaves that April day, it didn't instantaneously end my depression and bring me to a place of joy. But it stirred my desire to live. It enticed me to notice and pay attention to the world around me. And at a time when I felt hopeless, this moment of mystery gave me hope that there is more to life—my life, the life of the world— than usually meets the eye . . . or the ear or any of my physical senses. In the moments when the veil parts, we see the not-yet now, we glimpse the mystery and beauty at the heart of all that is; we see things as they really are and not as they usually appear. It is as if we, like the disciples, are half-asleep and dreaming until the glory of transfiguration overshadows us and we wake, for a moment, to mystery.

LIVING THE SEASON

....

The liturgical color of Ordinary Time:
green (growth)

When have you experienced the parting of the veil and glimpsed the glory of God? How did you feel in that moment? Have there been times in your life when you have experienced these glimpses of glory more often than you usually do? What was going on in your life at that time that made you more open to or aware of the presence of God with you?

When you sit down for a meal at home, light a green candle. In our family, we continue to use the Easter litany throughout this cycle of Ordinary Time.

Candlelighter: Christ is risen.

Everyone else: Alleluia! He is risen indeed!

Read Exodus 34:29-35 and 2 Corinthians 3:12–4:2 (readings for Transfiguration Sunday, year C). The image of the veil is prominent in these two passages. What role does this image play in the Exodus passage? How is that different from its role in 2 Corinthians? How is the veil related to Jesus' transfiguration?

Pray a breath prayer. A breath prayer is simply a short prayer, usually the length of one or two breaths, that you can recall with ease and that enables you (with lots of practice!) to pray without ceasing. I find my breath prayer helps me to be present in the moment at hand, to pay attention to where God might be present in that moment, and to be mindful of my desire to keep my eyes and heart turned toward Christ.

The Jesus Prayer—"Lord Jesus Christ, Son of God, have mercy on me, a sinner"—is a breath prayer that generations of Christians have found deeply meaningful. You can pray the Jesus Prayer or create your own short prayer that reflects your deepest desires for God's work in your life.[6]

Begin by choosing one activity that you do repeatedly (getting in a car, getting in an elevator, hanging up your phone) throughout the course of a given day. Each time you, say, wash your hands, pray your breath prayer. After doing this for a while, you will realize that every time you wash your hands, the breath prayer comes to mind without conscious effort. One task at a time, include the breath prayer in the routines of your life. Eventually you will find it seems to pray itself in you, allowing you to pray without ceasing and continually bringing your attention back to Christ.

Read 2 Peter 1:16-21 (epistle reading for Transfiguration Sunday, year A). What significance does Peter assign to the transfiguration? To what does he call his readers to be attentive? Why?

Conclusion

Full Circle: Christ the King

The church year begins with Advent, the longing of God's people for his appearance in our midst. Advent revolves slowly, quietly, into Christmas, a season of joy and celebration for the gift of God's Son, the Light of the world, born in human flesh. Christmas culminates in Epiphany, a day to remember that Christ came to draw all people to himself in love. An interlude of Ordinary Time follows, in which we have the opportunity to notice the Light shining in unexpected places, in the daily, ordinary moments of our lives.

On Ash Wednesday, the church year circles into its next cycle with the commencement of Lent, a season of darkness, a time to reckon with our mortality, our shortcomings, our sin. The darkness inaugurated with the mark of the ashes grows ever deeper through the weeks of Lent, reaching its nadir in the Triduum, the days of Jesus' betrayal, crucifixion and burial, before the light returns with great glory on Easter. We celebrate the resurrection of Jesus for fifty days, a season that surprises us with joy and life where we expected only sorrow and death. Easter culminates in Pentecost, a day to remember the gift of the Holy Spirit, the very presence of God with us, empowering us to be the body of Christ in the world. Another season of Ordinary Time follows, this one far longer than the first, in which our quotidian labors and relationships can lull us into a sleepy state of inattentiveness until those fragile, beautiful moments of transfiguration wake us to the blinding reality of God's nearness. These weeks of Ordinary Time come and go, ebb and flow, circling us ever nearer to the close of the year.

The last Sunday of the church year celebrates the kingship of Christ. As we end the year, it is only fitting to celebrate the eschatological reality that Christ will come again in power and glory to reign over all the earth.

Many people have issues with the language of kingship, perhaps because of its connotations of dominance, hierarchy and colonialism. I confess I am not among them. To my mind, Christ as King is comforting. The King who would come among his subjects to live as one of them and then allow them to execute him rather than calling on the power at his disposal—I see no dominance here, no hierarchy, no colonialism. I see only love.

On the Feast of Christ the King, we celebrate the day when Christ's great love will be fully realized on earth, the day when our King will return. He will right all wrongs. He will judge the living and the dead. He will bind up the brokenhearted. He will give sight to the blind. He will heal the lame. He will set the prisoners free. He will establish justice once and for all, justice tempered with mercy so that all life might flourish under his reign. It is this victorious coming that we celebrate on the final Sunday of the church year, a liturgical entering into the eschatological reality of Christ's return.

And so we have come full circle. We end the church year proclaiming and celebrating Christ's second coming. The next week, a new church year begins, and we circle into Advent again, living into our longing for God to come to us, crying with generations of God's people:

Come, Lord Jesus!

Appendix

Worshiping Throughout the Church Year:
Some Ideas for Worship Leaders

ADVENT/CHRISTMAS/EPIPHANY

- One way to practice the art of waiting is to refrain from singing Christmas carols during Advent. By Christmas carols, I mean songs that focus on the birth or arrival of Jesus—"Joy to the World," for instance, or "Away in a Manger." Songs that focus on the *coming* of Jesus, like "O Come, O Come Emmanuel," are perfectly themed for Advent. In some church traditions such songs are called Advent carols.

  If you're in a position to influence your church's choice of hymns or worship songs, encourage the music director to refrain from selecting Christmas carols during Advent. At my church, the music director insists on this. One Advent Sunday, the children's speaker, Tim, wanted to teach the kids the story of the composition of "Silent Night" and then sing it together, accompanying them on his guitar. When the music director found out about this plan, he asked Tim not to sing the carol. So, just as all the kids were about to begin singing, Tim stopped strumming and said, "Wait! It's not Christmas yet is it? Well, this is a Christmas carol, so we're going to have to wait until Christmas to sing it!" Then he dismissed the kids to their classes, as laughter rippled among the adults in the pews. Tim taught not just the children but also the adults that Christmas carols are for Christmas. Two weeks later, during Christmas, he was back, and this time the kids did sing "Silent Night."

- Make a point of singing Christmas carols during the church services on the two Sundays after Christmas as a way of savoring a "long, slow Christmas."

- Host a "house blessing" for your church, following a liturgy similar to the one outlined in chapter three.

LENT/EASTER/PENTECOST

- One of the loveliest, and simplest, Lenten fasts is the corporate "goodbye to alleluia." During the weeks leading up to Easter, it is customary in liturgical churches to refrain from saying or singing *alleluia* when we gather in worship. This simple fast is a way of marking the season of Lent as a time set apart, a time unlike any other in the Christian year. It furthermore serves to highlight and intensify the alleluias that will be said on Easter morning and throughout the Easter season when we proclaim Jesus' resurrection. If your church does not yet embrace this practice, consider incorporating the "goodbye to alleluia."

- At my church, it is an Easter Day tradition to sing the "Hallelujah Chorus" from Handel's *Messiah* at the end of each service. Congregants who wish to join in singing are invited to come to the choir loft, where sheet music is available and everyone squeezes in—usually about a third of the folks in the pews crowd into the choir to sing. Amazingly, this impromptu choir always sounds incredible. It is especially meaningful because we have fasted from saying and singing alleluia for all of Lent.

- Include the Easter greeting at some point in the service each Sunday of the season. (The congregation responds to the leader with the words in italics.)

Christ is risen!
He is risen indeed!
Christ is risen!
He is risen indeed!
Christ is risen!
Alleluia! He is risen indeed!

- On Pentecost, read Scripture in different languages. At my church this tradition has had many iterations: one person reading a passage in Spanish or Chinese or French or Swahili; people reading the same passage at the same time in different languages; people reading one passage a verse at a time, each verse in a different language.
- Decorate the church with red cloth. If you can have it hanging from the ceiling, draped over a cross or otherwise falling down above the heads of the congregation, so much the better to remind everyone present of the descent of the Holy Spirit.
- Host a Festival of Gifts. The Spirit gave the followers of Jesus the ability not just to speak in other languages but also to heal, prophesy, teach, preach, interpret and serve. As Christians, we believe that *all* our gifts and talents come from God. For many years at my church we celebrated these gifts on Pentecost with

a Festival of Gifts. The Fellowship Hall became an art gallery with paintings, quilts, flower arrangements, sculpture and other displays of artistic talent. There were poetry and story readings, music and dance performances, and a picnic on the lawn. Such a venue gave many in our church whose gifts did not "fit" in the context of Sunday morning worship the opportunity to be recognized and celebrated.

Resources for the Church Year

Selected Books for Further Reading

This is by no means an exhaustive list. The books listed below are ones I have found helpful, interesting, thought-provoking and sometimes inspiring.

Bread and Wine: Readings for Lent and Easter. Farmington, Penn.: Plough Publishing House, 2003, and *Watch for the Light: Readings for Advent and Christmas.* Farmington, Penn.: Plough Publishing House, 2001. These two books provide thematically appropriate readings from great Christian spiritual writers for each day of Advent and Christmas, Lent and Easter.

Kelly, Joseph F. *The Origins of Christmas.* Collegeville, Minn.: Liturgical Press, 2004. A fascinating account of how Christmas came to be dated and of the origins of many of the images and traditions associated with this holy day.

L'Engle, Madeleine. *The Irrational Season.* New York: Harper-SanFrancisco, 1977. One of The Crosswicks Journals, this thought-provoking book follows the structure of the church year as L'Engle ramblingly meditates on what it means to be human.

Nelson, Gertrud Mueller. *To Dance with God: Family Ritual and Community Celebration.* New York: Paulist, 1986. An excellent handbook for incorporating the church year into family and community life.

Norris, Kathleen. *The Quotidian Mysteries: Laundry, Liturgy and "Women's Work."* New York: Paulist, 1998. This thought-provoking book, originally a lecture, is a treasure trove of wisdom about the role of daily activities in contributing to spiritual growth.

Purcell, Steven. *Even Among These Rocks.* Brewster, Mass.: Paraclete, 2001. A quiet and lovely book of quotations and the author's art and meditations on Lent, all beautifully hand-lettered.

Stewart, Sonja M., and Jerome W. Berryman. *Young Children and Worship.* Louisville, Ky.: Westminster John Knox, 1989. Centered around the church year and the stories of Scripture, this worship curriculum for three- to eight-year-olds enables young children to enter experientially into the seasons of the church year and the stories they tell. The introduction is especially rich and includes an excellent (though brief) overview of the church year.

Wright, Wendy M. *The Vigil: Keeping Watch in the Season of Christ's Coming.* Nashville: Upper Room, 1992; *The Rising: Living the Mysteries of Lent, Easter, and Pentecost.* Nashville: Upper Room, 1994; *The Time Between: Cycles and Rhythms in Ordinary Time.* Nashville: Upper Room, 1999. Evocative and beautifully written, this trilogy weaves together history, art, literature and the author's lived experience as she mines the theological and spiritual riches of the church year.

Zimmerman, Martha. *Celebrating the Christian Year.* Minneapolis: Bethany House, 1994. A Bible-focused approach to celebrating the church year, this book includes lots of practical ideas for incorporating these seasons into family life.

An excellent source of family and church resources for the church year is Liturgy Training Publications (www.ltp.org). We have used their Advent/Christmas calendar and accompanying devotional, "Fling Wide the Doors," for years. They also have Lent and Easter calendars.

Acknowledgments

I wish to gratefully acknowledge the many people who made it possible for me to write this book through their hospitality, their encouragement, their words of wisdom and their faith in me:

Lynne Baab, my patron saint of writing, put me in touch with her editor at InterVarsity Press, helped me plot out how to write the book, answered my questions about the writing/publishing process, encouraged me when the work began to feel fruitless and prayed for me—without ceasing, I do believe.

Anne Baumgartner, Jill Bell, Glyn Devereaux, Janette Plunkett, Mike Purdy and many others shared stories of how they and their families try to live the church year. Their experiences made this a richer book.

Dianne Ross's affirmation and enthusiasm about this book early in its formation, when I was feeling rather despondent about my ability to write it, came at the exact moment I most needed words of encouragement.

Dave Zimmerman, my editor at InterVarsity Press, who seems to delight in putting himself out on a limb, took a big risk by advocating for an unknown writer. His encouragement, graciousness and sense of humor throughout the revising of my manuscript kept me from despairing over its flaws.

Mike Purdy, whose careful reading and thoughtful comments, especially on the Advent and Christmas chapters, made this a much better book than it would otherwise have been, generously allowed me to steal some of his sentences and claim them as my own.

Anne Baumgartner, Elizabeth Edwards, Cathee Kneeling and Matt Swanson read the book in an early version and provided helpful feedback about where it worked and where it needed work.

Susan Forshey, friend and fellow pilgrim, encouraged and exhorted me. Her excitement when I got my book contract was equal only to my own.

Lisa Etter and the staff of Green Bean Coffeehouse, where most of this book was written, made me endless cups of steamed milk and welcomed me with unstinting hospitality.

Kimbra Hitch faithfully cared for my children, welcoming them into her heart and her life, giving me the time I needed to write.

My parents, Carol and Chris Conway, "published" my first book when I was six. Together with my sister, Jeniferlyn Conway Barrow, they have faithfully believed in me and my writing for as long as I can remember—even when it was abominably bad.

Last but never least (in God's economy the last are first, after all), my husband, Doug Ireton, has had constant faith in me as a writer, putting his money where his mouth was: his insistence that we pay for childcare so I could have devoted writing time each week made it possible for me to write this book. His feedback about the earliest version of the book was invaluable—I'm not sure how he managed to be both honest and kind about such a mess, but he was, and I'm so grateful.

Notes

INTRODUCTION: ENTERING THE CIRCLE

[1]For several years in my faith journey, I would have been loath to use the masculine pronoun to refer to God (unless, of course, I was talking specifically about Jesus). The exclusive use of *he, him* and *his* to talk about God has unfortunately given many people the heretical idea that God is male or the equally heretical idea that if "he" is not male, then "he" is more male than female, or more like a man than a woman. This is not an issue I intend to address here, other than to acknowledge the danger of using masculine pronouns. I have chosen to do so primarily because not using a pronoun is often awkward. While most of this awkwardness can be alleviated by rewording or reworking a sentence, there are instances where no amount of fiddling can eradicate the inherent awkwardness of a phrase like "God's self." Many people embrace this language. For a while, I did too. But my love of beauty and simplicity, especially in written language, eventually outweighed my objections to the masculine pronoun *himself,* which this phrase was created to replace. I will therefore use masculine pronouns in reference to God throughout this book, though I do so as sparingly as possible.

CHAPTER 1: ADVENT

[1]Different churches sometimes use different watchwords and biblical figures. The ones I use here are among the most common. The third Sunday is an exception; it is almost universally associated with Mary and with joy.

[2]Based on the *Revised Common Lectionary.* The Gospel passages for the first Sunday of Advent are Matthew 24:36-44 (year A), Mark 13:24-37 (year B) and Luke 21:25-36 (year C).

[3]Henri Nouwen, "Waiting for God," in *Watch for the Light: Readings for Advent and Christmas* (Farmington, Penn.: Plough Publishing House, 2001), November 28.

[4]An Advent wreath usually consists of one pink candle and three purple candles, one for each of the four weeks of Advent. (The pink candle is for the third week.) Often in the center of the wreath there is a white candle, the Christ candle, which remains unlit until Christmas Eve.

[5]*Book of Common Worship: Daily Prayer* (Louisville, Ky.: Westminster John Knox, 1993), p. 33.

[6]I pieced this passage together from the NRSV and the Book of Common Worship.

[7]Nouwen, "Waiting for God," November 28.

CHAPTER 2: CHRISTMAS

[1]For the European, North African, Middle Eastern and Cappadocian forebears in faith to whom I refer here, December 25 was very nearly the winter solstice. I recognize that the theological and symbolic reasons I cite here hold true only in the Northern Hemisphere.

[2]Wendy M. Wright, *The Vigil: Keeping Watch in the Season of Christ's Coming* (Nashville: Upper Room, 1992), p. 77.

[3]Johannes Tauler, quoted in ibid.

[4]Wright, *The Vigil*, p. 77.

[5]In some parts of the Eastern Orthodox Church, Christmas is celebrated on January 6. In the West this holy day is associated with the coming of the Magi.

[6]Wright, *The Vigil*, p. 80.

[7]Fleming Rutledge, *The Bible and The New York Times* (Grand Rapids: Eerdmans, 1998), p. 58.

CHAPTER 3: EPIPHANY

[1]Fleming Rutledge, *The Bible and The New York Times* (Grand Rapids: Eerdmans, 1998), p. 62.

[2]Ibid., p. 65.

[3]Wendy M. Wright, *The Vigil: Keeping Watch in the Season of Christ's Coming* (Nashville: Upper Room, 1992), p. 161.

[4]For this insight into the twinned themes of Epiphany, I am indebted to Wendy Wright. See pp. 161-67 of *The Vigil*.

[5]Wright, *The Vigil*, p. 161.

[6]Dr. Bruce Murphy gave this illustration in a sermon he preached at Bethany Presbyterian Church, Seattle, Washington, sometime between 1994 and 1997.

[7]William Barclay, *The Gospel of John*, vol. 2 (chaps. 8-21), rev. ed. (Philadelphia: Westminster Press, 1975), p. 109.

[8]Chalk- and house-blessings are adapted from Gertrud Mueller Nelson, *To Dance with God: Family Ritual and Community Celebration* (New York: Paulist, 1986), pp. 118-20.

CHAPTER 4: ORDINARY TIME

[1]Wendy M. Wright, *The Time Between: Cycles and Rhythms in Ordinary Time* (Nashville: Upper Room, 1999), p. 9.

[2]In Orthodox churches in which Christmas is celebrated on January 6, the Presentation is celebrated on February 15. In some Protestant churches, it is celebrated on the Sunday closest to February 2 (between January 28 and February 3).

[3]Kathleen Norris, *The Cloister Walk* (New York: Riverhead Books, 1996), p. 114.

CHAPTER 5: LENT

[1]A caution: fasting from all food is not for everyone. Women who are pregnant or breastfeeding, people with diabetes, and anyone with a history of eating disorders should refrain from total food fasts. People with other medical conditions should consult their physicians before fasting from food.

[2]Lynne Baab, *Fasting: Spiritual Freedom Beyond Our Appetites* (Downers Grove, Ill.: InterVarsity Press, 2006), p. 28.

[3]Tim Dearborn and Don Posterski <www.dynamiscourse.com>.

[4]All the Scripture quoted in this section is from the King James Version.

[5]Wendy M. Wright, *The Rising: Living the Mysteries of Lent, Easter, and Pentecost* (Nashville: Upper Room, 1994), p. 110.

[6]Ibid., p. 111.

CHAPTER 6: EASTER

[1]Technically, Easter falls on the first Sunday after the "paschal moon," which is based on the Jewish lunar calendar. Churches in the East use a nineteen-year cycle for determining the date of the paschal moon; Western churches use an eighty-four-year cycle. Furthermore, the Eastern Orthodox Church uses the Julian calendar (versus the Gregorian calendar in the West) and also requires that Easter fall after Passover, whereas in the West it can occur weeks before Passover. Thus, the date of Easter is often different in the East and West.

[2]Wendy M. Wright, *The Rising: Living the Mysteries of Lent, Easter, and Pentecost* (Nashville: Upper Room, 1994), p. 111.

[3]Ibid., pp. 117-18.

[4]Luke 24:13-49, which is the lectionary reading for Easter evening each year.

[5]I am indebted to Jeff VanDuzer for this insight into the role of encounter with the risen Christ in effecting transformation among his followers. "On the Road to Emmaus," sermon, Bethany Presbyterian Church, Seattle, Washington, April 15, 2007.

[6]Wright, *The Rising*, p. 162.

[7]Gertrud Mueller Nelson, *To Dance with God: Family Ritual and Community Celebration* (New York: Paulist, 1986), p. 182.

CHAPTER 7: PENTECOST

[1]C. S. Lewis, *Prince Caspian: The Return to Narnia* (New York: Scholastic, 1951), pp. 157-58.

[2]Ibid., p. 158.

[3]Ibid., pp. 198-99.

[4]Ibid., p. 160.

[5]These words are from Godly Play, a liturgy-based educational program for children. (See Sonja Stewart and Jerome Berryman's book in the resources list for more information.) Before reading the Scripture passage for the day, the worship leader lights the Christ candle and says, "We light the Christ candle to remind us that God is with us in a special way when we read the Bible." At the end of the liturgy, she snuffs out the candle, moving the snuffer in a half-circle in front of her so the smoke can drift toward each of the children, and says, "We change the light to remind us that God is with us in all times and all places." Because of the Holy Spirit, God indeed is with us all the time, everywhere.

CHAPTER 8: ORDINARY TIME

[1]L. M. Montgomery, *Emily of New Moon* (Toronto: Bantam, 1983), p. 7.

[2]For the story of the transfiguration, see Luke 9:28-36 (also Matthew 17:1-9 and Mark 9:2-10).

[3]See Exodus 14:24; 33:7-9; Numbers 12:5, 10; Deuteronomy 31:15.

[4]Kathleen Norris, *The Quotidian Mysteries: Laundry, Liturgy, and "Women's Work"* (New York: Paulist, 1998), p. 82.

[5]Ibid., p. 35.

[6]For detailed instructions on creating your own breath prayer, see Marjorie Thompson, *SoulFeast: An Invitation to the Christian Spiritual Life* (Louisville, Ky.: Westminster John Knox, 1995), pp. 47-49.

LIKEWISE. *Go and do.*

A man comes across an ancient enemy, beaten and left for dead. He lifts the wounded man onto the back of a donkey and takes him to an inn to tend to the man's recovery. Jesus tells this story and instructs those who are listening to "go and do likewise."

Likewise books explore a compassionate, active faith lived out in real time. When we're skeptical about the status quo, Likewise books challenge us to create culture responsibly. When we're confused about who we are and what we're supposed to be doing, Likewise books help us listen for God's voice. When we're discouraged by the troubled world we've inherited, Likewise books encourage us to hold onto hope.

In this life we will face challenges that demand our response. Likewise books face those challenges with us so we can act on faith.